VIETNAM
THROUGH
ROSE-COLORED
GLASSES

By RICHARD S. ROSE

MASTER CHIEF JOURNALIST, U.S. NAVY (RETIRED)

ISBN: 0615695027

ISBN-13: 9780615695020

DEDICATION

This book is dedicated to my late wife, Barbara, and to my daughter, Debbi, who experienced their own anxieties during my absence. After I returned from Vietnam and they read some of my news stories, they experienced some annoyance at my having gone places they felt I shouldn't have. They had assumed I was sitting safely in a Saigon office, sending others out into the Delta.

I couldn't do that. Or, at least, I couldn't *just* do that. A leader, and good or bad, I was that, has to experience what his subordinates (I prefer the word *colleagues*) did. So, this book is also dedicated to my colleagues, especially Photographer's Mate First Class Dan Dodd, who accompanied me on almost every mission.

Also, as with my previous book, *Tarnished Brass Curtain: A Novel of Vietnam,* it is dedicated to the men of the Brown Water Navy, those who manned the river boats and the helicopter crews who provided their support. I suppose, in keeping with the bitter humor in some articles, I also dedicate this to the late presidents, Lyndon Johnson and Richard Nixon, their cabinet officials and to the often clueless General Westmoreland, without whom there might not have been a Vietnam War.

I would be remiss if I didn't include the anti-war protesters and the VVAW, the Vietnam Veterans Against the War. They, too, were distant colleagues. I close this dedication with the always valid motto, "Honor the warrior, not the war."

DICK ROSE
August 2012

INTRODUCTION

Publishing a book about Vietnam over forty years after I served there may seem like an exercise in futility. And yet, after all this time, Vietnam still remains a history mystery. What was it about? Who will be interested in it? Vietnam vets? Of course. Vets of other wars? Who knows? History students? Hopefully, yes.

This book is definitely not a history. It is meant to be a collection of my views—some serious, some humorous, some in no category at all. It is, as the title says, through my eyes, *Through Rose-Colored Glasses*. It is definitely not impartial. I was there; I developed strong views; I exercised my sense of humor and, in some cases, my anger and frustration.

Some of it is contemporary to the time. Some of it was written years later in columns for the Vietnam Veterans of America (VVA) California State newspaper, *The California Zephyr*, and some for the VVA Chapter 419 newsletter, *Frontlines*.

My reasons for this book are three-fold: To share, to amuse, to record. As Col. Harry Summers, the late publisher and editor of the *Vietnam Magazine* (I think those were the names) said at one of the VVA National Conventions in the 1990's, "If you were an hour away or a klick[1] away, you were in a different war." I spent a lot of

1   *Kilometer; a click to adjust a gun sight for that distance)*

hours in a lot of places, and met a lot of people, so I experienced, perhaps, a lot of wars.

When I decided to assemble this book, the question came up: Do I update the articles or leave them as I wrote them at the time? I decided they were products of their time and my views at those times. As to the order of the entries, it is arbitrary, neither chronological nor ordered with any significance. My intent is not to educate but to share. Only the reader can determine my success.

TABLE OF CONTENTS

Why Vietnam 1

Orders. 5

Interview With a Sergeant 15

Vietnam As A Guilt-Edged Bond 19

A Parrot, A Projector 23
and a Carton of Cigarettes

Forty-Year Flashback. 27

Too Old 31

What Would We Do Without Jane Fonda?. 33

Choosing the Pain 37

The Corrosive Effects of Tarnished Brass. . . 41

Is the Vietnam War Irrelevant?. 45

You're History! 47

MacNamara's "Revelation" Reveals Little . . . 49

Poetry. 57

Fiction 73

And On The Seventh Day. 73

Another Hill To Be Taken. 89

Photographs 97

This was written in June of 1993, 25 years after I left Vietnam. I suppose in some way it encapsulates the reason for my having compiled this book and written my novel, "Tarnished Brass Curtain: A Novel of Vietnam." Needless to say, but I do say it, it still applies today, almost 20 years later, when I'm 81.

WHY VIETNAM?

Twenty-five years ago I served in Vietnam—and the memory remains. Why? Why does this one year dominate my life so? Why do I identify with Vietnam and not some other incident or place?

Forty years ago, April, 1953, I was in Japan, recovering from a minor scrape with the Marine MPs, having earned from it a concussion, a Summary Court Martial, a hold on my impending promotion and the deep admiration of my fellow "deck-apes" on the *USS Pollux*. That certainly was significant in my life, memorable, but that was 40 years ago, not 25, and it wasn't Vietnam. Vietnam remains.

Twenty-five years ago, in June,1968, Robert Kennedy was assassinated in Los Angeles, but I wasn't in Los Angeles. I was at a Special Forces camp at Thung Thoi, three miles from the Cambodian border. I was in Vietnam.

Twenty-two years ago, in February, I was at the Coronado, California, Naval Amphibious Base as senior enlisted member of the *USS Pueblo* Command Information Bureau, playing host to the world's news media. I was interviewed by "TIME Magazine," and subsequently featured in a third of a page profile, after which I was branded as a "senior enlisted hippie" by the Naval Amphibious

1

Force command chief of staff; earning for myself an invitation to retire as soon as possible, gaining a new awareness of the outside world, and the admiration of the junior officers and enlisted men on the staff. It was memorable. I was famous (for a brief time). I was preparing to embark on a civilian career, college, a world apart from the Navy. But it wasn't Vietnam. Vietnam remains.

Thirty years ago, in June, I was at Pt. Mugu, California, Naval Air Station, preparing for a visit from the President of the United States. As Air Force One landed, JFK came out and shook hand with those nearby; shook hands with the civilian crowd invited aboard the base; he shook my hand. It was an electric moment, one which gave me my first contact with that evanescence known as "personal magnetism." I remember that moment. I also remember chiding a member of the Secret Service who was "going ballistic" because I had stationed one of our photographers on the roof of the hangar. "Relax," I said in June of 1963, "who would shoot the President?" I remember that. That certainly remains. But it wasn't Vietnam.

Vietnam was where I celebrated my 37th birthday (normally, a most unmemorable birthday, but this one occurred in Vietnam.) Vietnam was where I spent my 13th anniversary, the first, last and only one away from my wife.

Vietnam was where I picked up a weapon for the first time in 16 years and got some immediate on-the-job training on the correct use of a .45 pistol and an M-16. Vietnam was where I unwound from an ambush op with the *Xung Kich* (Vietnam Regional Force Commandos trained by US Marines), by drinking too much beer, getting drunk and messing up the newly tarred entrance to the hooch of the commanding officer of the *Nha Be* Naval Base; this resulted in my being declared *persona non grata* at the base, earning me the admiration of Marine Advisory Team 43 and my co-workers back in Saigon (at least the junior officers and the enlisted men). That was Vietnam.

Saigon, Nha Be, Dan Nang, Vinh Long, Ben Tre, Thung Thoi, Chau Doc, the *Co Chien* and the *Bassac* Rivers, the Mekong Delta from the Cambodian border south. This was my Vietnam.

Three years ago I joined the Vietnam Veterans of America (VVA) and am now the president of San Fernando Valley Chapter 419. But, again, why VVA? For a brief time I was a member of the American Legion, but never attended a meeting (a co-worker at the IRS got points for signing me up.) I'm a Life Member of the Disabled American Veterans, but I never attended their meetings, either. And to be truthful, as a Korean War veteran, I'm closer in age to that group than to that of my VVA brothers. But even now, the stickers on the back of my two cars don't read "California" or UCLA," or "Korean Conflict Survivor" or even "Go, IRS!" They read "Vietnam Veteran" and "Vietnam Vet, Class of 68."

So, once again, why Vietnam? What hold does that one year have on me? I spent three years in Taiwan, almost six in Japan, and only one year in Vietnam. Fifty years ago I was in Chicago; thirty years ago I was at Pt. Mugu; twenty years ago I was in San Diego; fifteen years ago I was on a cruise ship in the Caribbean; Two years ago I was in San Francisco as a delegate to the VVA National Convention.

Every year for the past 60-something I've been somewhere... and nowhere. Why?

Because twenty-five years ago I was in Vietnam.

June 1993

Orders

Japan was its usual humid self in August of 1967 when I received *the* phone call. I was at my desk in the newsroom of the Far East Network (FEN), Tokyo. I may have been reviewing the next newscast, or I may have been thinking about our bowling team — the FENtastics.

Whatever I was thinking or doing is a lost memory. Because of **The Phone Call**. "Senior Chief Rose? This is Chief Personnelman (*and here, I admit, I forget the name of the Bearer of the News*), in Yokosuka. Your orders to Vietnam are in."

*My orders to Vietnam? I don't have any orders to Vietnam. I'm **not** expecting any orders to Vietnam.* (I refrained from immediately asking if it was a joke — just as I'd refrained entirely 10 months earlier on my last call from Yokosuka when I'd been told I was promoted to Senior Chief.) "Very funny, Chief. What did you really call me about? My tour here isn't up till next March."

"No, seriously, Chief. You have orders to Saigon, NAVFORV headquarters, with a transfer date no later than Aug. 31st."

"Chief. This *has* to be a joke." I don't give up easily. "I have a wife and daughter, and a houseful of furniture in Momote Village.

And, as I said, my tour isn't up until next March. How can this happen?"

"Senior Chief Rose. Remember getting promoted last October? Well, your billet at FEN doesn't call for a Senior Chief. So, you're available. And the Chief in Saigon cracked up and they need an immediate replacement."

"What about weapons training? I haven't touched a weapon since boot camp — and that was 16 years ago!" Visions of having to field strip a carbine at Camp Elliott in San Diego suddenly appeared before me. My left cheekbone began to sting with the remembered recoil from when I kept my face too close to whatever part of the gun it is that hits you in the face when you get your face too close to it.

"Don't worry about it Chief, I'm sure you'll get some OJT."

Great, OJT. On the job training in a war zone? There was a war going on! I knew that. After all, I was chief of the News Room. We were writing newscasts about it. *Saigon, Da Nang, Pleiku.* I knew all the names.

Not only that, but less than three months earlier, I spent a rather painful month-and-a-half in the 249th General Hospital at Camp Drake in the Officers Ward surrounded mostly by shot-up helicopter pilots. Before that, I'd been on the abdominal injury ward, surrounded mostly by paratroopers. I knew the effects of the war.

But accepting the inevitable, I realized that I was in for a very rough future — No, not going to Vietnam. As a writer, and a still-innocent patriot ...and a career military man, I could almost look forward to going to Vietnam. No, the most difficult thing I had to face was telling my wife.

Eleven years before, when I had re-enlisted (after having quit the Navy to marry her), I promised her we would never be separated. So far, I'd been right.

To tell or not to tell — that really *wasn't* a question. After a couple of months she would've noticed I wasn't around. The question was *How?*

The problem? How to tell my wife, Bobbie. For a moment, though, I had contemplated not telling her, but this would have been impossible to do.

I am not averse to attempting the impossible, but it was fairly obvious she'd have known something was up when the movers came to our little cottage in Momote Village at Camp Drake, and started to take our furniture.

Our furniture. That was the first problem. We were still having it made for us. And we had told the furniture maker we had a few months left. We had a 2-piece hutch, a buffet, a coffee table and a couple of end tables. Still to be made were our bedroom and dining room furniture. It appeared obvious I wasn't ready to be be transferred.

Not to San Diego, not to Naples (where I had [almost] been promised a billet), not to a ship, and, most definitely, not to Vietnam.

My thinking started to get jumbled (much like this column). Vietnam was calling me. And I had to tell my wife. So I made the first move. I went home.

When I walked in, I realized I had worried over nothing. I didn't have to tell her. She knew! As soon as I walked in and said "Hi!", she looked at me and asked, "What's wrong?"

"What makes you think something's wrong?" It had to be the "Hi." I never say "Hi."

"It shows on your face. What's wrong." A month short of my 12th anniversary, and my wife can read my face. What were the next 12 going to be like? (This scene was repeated a week later when our daughter, Debbi, returned from girl scout camp. She took one look at both our faces, and asked "What's wrong?")

But back to the then present. "I've got orders. We've got to leave by the end of the month."

"It's Vietnam, isn't it?" In retrospect, what else could it have been?

So, it wasn't that hard, after all (relatively speaking, and looking back 29 years). We went through the whole Kübler-Ross cycle — denial, anger, bargaining, grieving and, finally, acceptance. And we did it two years before Dr. K-R described it in her book!

Once Bobbie had accepted it, it was all hectic business. We had to arrange for picking up our household effects, telling our stateside families, arranging for Bobbie to move in with her mother, and shopping.

Suddenly, I was able to buy whatever I wanted. A new watch? No usual question — Do I really need it? I wanted it; it was mine. And I rode that train for as long as I could. I also got a new Pentax SLR. I tried for a Super-8 movie camera, but the ride didn't last that long. (I did get one, eventually, at the Cholon PX; but that was another world, and another story.)

We had to go to the Navy base at Yokosuka, forty miles south of Tokyo, where my personnel records were, and where I could order a couple of extra pairs of glasses, where I could get the necessary shots, and where I got another set of dog tags.

That precipitated another near-incident. When I gave the personnelman my vital details, he punched them in on the spot. He gave the dog-tags to me, and I handed them to Bobbie to put in her purse. She noticed they were shaped differently from the oval ones issued me in boot camp. "What's this notch on the edge?" she asked.

"Oh," said the idiot, "that where they push it into the teeth, to make the body easier to identify." That did it! Kübler-Ross revisited, with the emphasis on grief for her, and anger for me.

However, we survived that, too. And the three weeks left were so crammed with things to do, we didn't have a chance to think about Vietnam...yet. Other problems still awaited us. For instance, when we arrived at Travis Air Force Base from Japan, our luggage didn't. But lost luggage was really minor.

I was in the States. The following day was my 12th anniversary. And in ten days, I would be back at Travis.

Headed for Vietnam.

This was a book review I wrote for the Vietnam Veterans of America California State newspaper, "The California Zephy.r" It was selected as "Editorial of the Year."

Epiphanies

I had just finished reading a couple of long poems by a vet named Scott Morrison. One, "Froggie Went A'Colonizing," was a re-cap of the history of colonized Vietnam from France's entry to America's withdrawal; it consists of 60 verses, sung to the folk tune "Froggie A'Courtin'."

The other, "Gotta Save Pittsburgh," is a cadence-count satire of the need to destroy Vietnam to keep the commies off the Ohio River.

In his accompanying letter, Morrison describes his spiritual journey as a Goldwater conservative "rock-ribbed Republican" university student who, in 1968, decided to research the history of Vietnam and American involvement, so he could refute the anti-war activists, demonstrators and Canada-bound draft-eligibles.

11

His objective was a research paper he could use in two different government and political science classes. In the research, he discovered some truths which "turned [his] Republican rock-ribs to sand."

He refers to this as his personal epiphany. An interesting word, *epiphany*. The American Heritage Dictionary defines it as

3. a. A sudden manifestation of the essence or meaning of something. b. A comprehension or perception of reality by means of a sudden intuitive realization. [ME epiphanie < OFr. < LLat. epiphania < Gk. epiphaneia, appearance < epiphainein, to manifest : epi-, to + phainein, to show.]

The question, now, is: Do we all experience epiphanies? Does everyone discover a sudden truth in an instant? Were we aware of that moment of truth? Was it *truth*? I can ask these questions. I cannot answer them. Inherent in the definition, an epiphany is personal. Therefore, I can only answer for myself. The answer, for me, is *yes*!

My epiphany came in two parts – the doubt and the realization. It was an instant revelation whose two parts were separated by about six weeks. *Doubt* came on my second day in-country, September, 1967. I was given a two-day indoctrination in Saigon – precautions, dangers, local customs, and a warning by the Army sergeant conducting the indoctrination.

"Remember this," he said, "when you're out there on the streets any man, woman or child could be the enemy." I suppose he gave that warning to everyone. On the face of it, it's practical, it's common sense...it's disturbing! If any man, woman, or child here, in Saigon, capital of the Republic of Vietnam, could be the enemy, I asked myself, were we there as liberators or as occupiers?

That was the beginning of doubt. And Doubt was not welcome. I was, after all, a senior chief petty officer, a veteran of 16 years in the Navy, a former news editor for the Far East Network, a purveyor of truth. I should have no doubts about my country's mission.

But I did.

Epiphany, Part II, came about a month later. I was researching and writing a story about a HA(L) 3 detachment, a Navy helicopter unit working with Operation Game Warden out of *Vinh Long*, on *the Co Chien* branch of the Mekong River.

We had just finished shooting up some people in a Free Fire Zone. "How," I asked the pilot, "do we know that those people we just shot up were VC?" (Hell, I was a journalist; I asked questions.)

"Because we killed them," he answered me on the ship's intercom.

BINGO! *Epiphanysville*. We don't kill people because they're the enemy. They're the enemy because we killed them. Because, I guess, like Mt. Everest, they were there. They were not merely fisherman who may have found a fruitful supply on an unused small river; they were where they didn't belong; they were killed; they were the enemy.

This was a piece of military logic even I, with my 16 years' experience, hadn't grasped. Descartes would have been thrilled. No longer was it *I think; therefore I am*. It was now *You die; therefore you are VC*.

My two-part epiphany was now complete: Any man, woman, or child, if you kill him, her, or it, is the enemy. Now, finally, no more doubt.

After all, I'd had an epiphany.

1994

When I was still at the Far East Network Newsroom, I expressed my disappointment with the feature news coming out of Vietnam in the "Stars & Stripes". One of my co-workers, a Marine sergeant, asked me if I could do better. I didn't know.

However, in June I was in the Army's 249th General Hospital, where the wounded were sent before being sent back to the States. I talked to many of the troops, from some paratroopers with stomach wounds to helicopter pilots when I was moved to the Junior Officers' ward. This gave me the chance to write the following. The Marine sergeant agreed I could do and did better than what was in "Stars & Stripes."

Interview With A Sergeant

So you want an interview.
You want to know what War is like;
What I feel and what I think;
How I lead my men.

Have you ever been in a war?
I didn't think so!
If you had, you wouldn't ask;
You couldn't ask.
But you did ask, so I'll try to explain.
Maybe I can understand, myself.
And understand myself.

To begin with, I'd say it's Duty—
Or, a better word, Order.
A matter of my being ordered into combat
As a soldier
To restore order in the chaos—
In order to have Peace.
And you, an information specialist,
Ordered to interview me in this hospital.

You sit here, a thousand miles from combat
And try to imagine our feelings.
And you can.
But you can never feel our
Imaginings!

You want to interview me?
Okay, but we'll talk about you.
You sit here and feel guilty
Because I've been wounded,
And you haven't fired a weapon
Since basic training.

So you're extra nice to a
Grouchy guy like me,
And you ignore my rudeness.

But you shouldn't regret not going
Any more than I regret going.
You've got your orders
And I have mine,
And we'll have some in the future.
And we'll both do them without regrets
Because the good soldier is never sorry,
And the sorry soldier is never good.

What's War like?
Ask the kid there is the next bed.
He'll tell you that it's fear.
At first, you're afraid of being afraid;
And then you taste the real fear, itself,
As you look for an enemy who's looking for you
And you both secretly hope you'll never meet.
And then, one day,
You're no longer afraid,
And that scares you even more
Because then you're afraid
Of yourself.

Or ask one of the other guys.
Any one – or all.
They'll tell you

War is Nature turned around.
In the middle of the day
It's dark with fear.
In the middle of the night, it's
Bright with hope.
Sometimes.

Or you can suddenly be cold
In the jungle heat—
Cold and dark and all alone.
Or you can be hot
In the chill of the night.
It doesn't make sense.
But War never does.

Ask any one the men here
What War is like,
And they'll all give you the same answers
Which will all be different.
Ask 'em again, and
They'll all give you different answers,
Which will all be the same.
Ask me.

What's War like?
Don't ask.
I hope you never find out.

249th General Hospital, Camp Drake, Japan, 1967

Vietnam as a
Guilt-Edged Bond

Late in October, 1994, around Harvest Moon time, Chapter 419 President Ed Hedrick and I attended the VVA National Leadership Conference in Denver, so we could, among other things, pick up a few pointers for getting the chapter moving.

We attended meetings, training sessions, project seminars, and an awards luncheon. It was, as it was meant to be, educational and enlightening.

On the last evening, when there was nothing scheduled, I went down to the lobby of the hotel and mingled with members from other chapters, other states. This was educational, too, in a serendipitous way.

Perhaps it was the moon, or the mood, or the calm after a three fast-paced days, but the aura was one of retrospection. Of course, anything to do with Vietnam is retrospective, and introspective. That's what draws us together—shared experiences, with the perverse realization that we all had different experiences which cannot be shared.

What I saw, what I heard, was a sense of regret, a sense of loss, of lack of completion. Everyone, including me, seemed to feel guilty about something. For me it was triggered by some guys at a piano singing about Saigon Commandos, colloquially known as *REMF*s. I suppose that was how I view myself.

Sure, I wasn't in Saigon all the time. I did some time on the river patrol boats, on attack helicopters, and even a memorable ambush op with some Vietnamese commandos (*Xung Kich*) and their *Semper Fi* advisors. But that wasn't enough. Other navymen were on the river 12-14 hours a day, 7 days a week. Others flew combat patrol missions every day. I only did it a few times. It's what kept me from joining VVA much sooner. I didn't feel I belonged.

I felt guilty. But I didn't realize that others who had done all those things I hadn't done also felt guilty. They didn't do as many missions as others, or as long a mission as a buddy did, or encounter as much hostile fire, or get wounded, or even get killed.

This last was brought to my attention with a poem called *The Missing Name*, in the Chapter 526 Newsletter, where the writer regrets his name in not on the wall next to that of his buddy.

And then there's the guilt felt by those who served during the era, but not in-country. And at least one associate member expressed his regret that he wasn't old enough to have served (his father did).

Perhaps this is what the psychologists call *Survivor's Guilt*. Or perhaps not

Is it *guilt, regret, reminiscence, nostalgia,* or *None of the Above.* Is it something for which I have an answer, since I've posed the question? Absolutely not! Am I playing with words, with memories, with ideas? Perhaps. I don't know.

I do know that there was something there, amid the cigarette smoke and the piano music, amid the clinking of glasses at the bar and the camaraderie, amid the singing of old songs and the quiet conversations.

What was it? Was it all part of a guilt-edged bond we all share? Or was it all only the Harvest Moon?

January 1995

A PARROT, A PROJECTOR AND A CARTON OF CIGARETTES

I hope the Statute of Limitations has run out because I have a confession to make. In 1967 I traded on Saigon's open and famous Black Market. Anyone who was in Saigon back then couldn't help but notice that these were everywhere, including (I believe) in front of the USO.

They were innocuous enough. Film, cigarettes, toothpaste and a slew of other common items, including one item that the PX (Post Exchange) was strangely always out of—*Bubble Up*, Coca Cola's calorie-free carbonated citrus drink of the 60s. These Black Market displays were strung out along the curbs of the major streets, unmolested by the authorities. But I never bought anything from them, not even my precious *Bubble Up*.

If the PX was out of it, then I just didn't buy any. The Cholon PX, in the Chinese section, was a very popular place, especially for the civilian contractors and the Korean soldiers, eager to spend their American dollars on cameras and mini-refrigerators. I suspect there must have been a Korean soldier permanently located

23

at the PX, because as soon as a refrigerator became available, the place was flooded with Korean soldiers buying every one available.

However, I was lucky enough to be there when a shipment did arrive, so I had one in my quarters in Saigon. All it took to live lavishly in pre-Tet Saigon was a fridge and an electric frying pan. In that pan I could fry an egg, cook up some macaroni and cheese, or heat up a can of soup.

Even so, there were occasional arguments over the items in short supply at the PX. I was there once when there was a Super-8 movie projector on display. I asked the clerk for it. While it was on the counter, an Army sergeant came up and said he wanted it. "Sorry," I said, "but I'm already buying it."

That didn't satisfy him. He looked me over and saw what he thought was a Navy Chief Petty Officer. "When did you make E-7?" he asked.

"1962," I replied.

"Well, I made E-7 in 1960, so I have seniority. I want that projector."

I tried being reasonable. "This PX usually works on a 'first come, first served basis. Rank shouldn't count."

"Well, I still want that projector." He was being stubborn.

"When did you make E-8?" I asked.

"I'm not an E-8."

"Well, I am. I made it last year." That seemed to resolve the issue as he walked away, mumbling a few curses about the F—ing Navy.

But, I should get back to my Black Market trading. I was at the PX one day when there was a young boy with a beautiful, and apparently tame, parrot on his shoulder standing across the street. I stopped to admire it.

"I give it you for carton cigarettes," he said. This was an offer too good to turn down. I went back across the street and into the PX. Since I don't smoke, I had to ask where the cigarettes were. Then I picked up a carton and went to the check-out counter.

"You're allowed to buy two cartons a week, you know," the clerk said. But I didn't want two cartons of cigarettes. I didn't even want one carton of cigarettes. I wanted a parrot. So, I paid for my one carton and was back across the street. Both boy and parrot were still there. I looked around but no one seemed to be paying attention, so we made our trade. There I was, a Senior Chief Petty Officer, committing an illegal act in the daylight, in the open.

I hurried back across the street with my precious cargo and boarded a MAC-V (Military Assistance Command-Vietnam) shuttle bus to go back to my billet. No one paid the least bit of attention to my strange cargo. I debarked (disembarked? got off?) across the street from my quarters, the Plaza Hotel, where the senior NCOs (non-commissioned officers) were housed, my home when I wasn't in the Mekong Delta.

I didn't get very far in before I was stopped by the Army Sergeant who ran the place. Apparently, I wasn't as invisible as I thought. "What the f— is that?"

"It's a parrot. I bought it in town." No sense mentioning the price.

"Well, you can't bring it in here. I'm confiscating it. Give it to me."

"What are you going to do with it?"

"That's not your concern. You can't keep it."

So all my illegal activity came to naught. I was out both a parrot and the price of a carton of cigarettes. All I had, and still have, is the memory of the failed crime and a good story to tell.

August, 2011

FORTY-YEAR FLASHBACK

Forty years ago, I was a young, newly-striped Navy Journalist Third Class (E-4). It had been a long wait, and I was proud of that stripe. I was now a petty officer, though still the junior man in our office. What it meant, other than more pay and a rank designation was unclear. For a while.

As I remember, it was late May, 1954, just after lights out in the barracks at the Yokosuka (Japan) Naval Base. I was reading in my bunk, when suddenly the lights came on, again. An officer stood by the switch. Someone yelled, "Attention on deck!" and we all jumped up.

"I want to see all petty officers assembled in front of the building in ten minutes," he announced. (*Wow!!! All petty officers. No seamen. No E-3s and below, just petty officers. Suddenly, my stripe mattered!*)

Ten minutes later, we were assembled in front of the building. I was wearing my dungarees, my press-on JO3 badge still stiff on my left sleeve. There were three Navy buses on the street which we were directed to board. We did.

We were taken to a hangar at the far corner of the base, overlooking the bay and the Oppama helicopter field on the other side. We off-loaded from the buses and marched (more or less) inside.

Once we were all in, the doors were closed behind us. Slammed noisily, as hangar doors usually are.

In front of us, as best as I can recall this many years later, were six long rows of tables. In the best military fashion, we were informed that there were six tables. (This, I assume, was for those of us who couldn't count. Though it seems to me that **counting** is sort of a requirement to be a petty officer.)

I cannot quote our orders, verbatim, but the essence was simple and clear:

- each tabled contained stacks of the same items;
- there were boxes at the beginning of each table. (These were about four inches high and twelve inches square.)
- Those of us who weren't detailed to put the boxes together were to take an assembled box, walk along the table, take one item from each stack, and put it in the box.
- We were to work as quickly as possible, were not to read the documents (a direct invitation to do exactly that, of course), and, most importantly, we were not to talk to each other, nor were we to discuss this after we left.

It was impressed upon us that this was a classified project and all of the materials were secret. The next morning, when we were finally dismissed,we were told to forget everything we had seen. Surprisingly, I did so. For many years. I'm hoping that it's been declassified since then. If not, this is being revealed in print for the first time.

You can blame the Navy for this. No one back then even checked to see if I was cleared for classified information. As a matter of fact, I wasn't. As the child of immigrants from Hungary, with the possibility of still having relatives living behind the iron curtain, I hadn't been worth the military's going to the trouble of a background check. (I didn't get one for another eight years, when I was a Chief Petty Officer assigned to the staff of the Pacific Missile Range Commander at Point Mugu.)

However, back to 1954. With all of the warnings about not looking, of course I looked at the stuff we were putting in the boxes. It was quite a collection:

- maps of Hanoi and Haiphong;
- lists of edible fruits and berries in the jungle;
- a cloth badge with an American flag and some foreign writing which I guessed was Vietnamese (those maps of Hanoi and Haiphong were a giveaway). I wouldn't have recognized Vietnamese in a thousand years (though I did, thirteen years later);
- a list of local contacts with addresses in Hanoi, Haiphong and other cities whose names I really do forget; and
- a few other items and documents whose significance were so unknown to me that I cannot, now, remember what they were, although I'm sure there were various medications, also.

I had seen enough World War II movies to know that the cloth patch was probably for the back of a flight jacket, and other information was enough so I knew these were some sort of combat packs for pilots. I was a steady reader of *Pacific Stars&Stripes* in Japan, so I knew that the French were in trouble in Vietnam and had already asked for American help. I'd guessed that this was it. Afterwards, in the barracks, we talked about it (a couple of us, at least, not totally unaware of the world outside the local bars and bath houses). We could see that we were preparing to help the French, and probably invade Vietnam after the flyboys softened them up.

That's what we guessed. The only thing is, it didn't happen. No pilots flying or being shot down over Hanoi, no invasion, no nothing. At least not then, not in 1954.

And so, as instructed, I forgot about it. For a while. If the memory recurred, it was on a sub-conscious level as I reported the news in the mid 1960s, from my post as chief of the Far East Network, Tokyo, newsroom. Hanoi, Haiphong, Vietnam in general, all were part of our news.

Then I was promoted to Senior Chief Journalist (E-8), and lost that job; I was back on the Vietnam track — August 1967 orders to Saigon with less than 30 days to report. Hanoi, Haiphong, etc., were to take on a closer meaning.

But what happened in 1954? What happened to all those packages I had put together? Why weren't they used? Years later, I learned that although Vice President Nixon and some military officers favored our aiding the French at Dien Bien Phu, President Eisenhower blocked it. He said he knew the American people would never support his sending troops to bail out the French trying to hold on to a colony.

Had he not, would the whole U.S. history have been different? Would I have ended up in Saigon in 1967? Earlier? Not at all?

Quien sabe? Wer weisst? Who knows?

1994

Too Old?

This month's column is only indirectly about Vietnam. It goes along with my having been twice the age of the average man who served in Vietnam (the average was about 18-1/2 years old. I was 36 when I arrived in country.)

In a moment of unexpected, and not exactly welcomed, burst of honesty, [the president of our Vietnam Veterans chapter] Ed Hedrick told me that he had been discussing me with someone at the last State Council meeting, and they had realized I was one of the oldest VVA members in California. Apparently, there aren't too many Korean War vets who are also VVA-eligible.

As I say, that wasn't exactly welcome news, though, I don't know why it surprises me. If anyone knows how old I am, certainly I know.

Our esteemed editor, my daughter Debbi, once said I may be the only person ever to go from adolescence to senility without achieving maturity. Perhaps I believe her. I'm in no rush to grow up. After 20 years in the Navy, 8½ years with the VA and another 13½ with the IRS, I still haven't figured out what I want to be when I grow up.

To get back to Vietnam, I arrived there as a Senior Chief Petty Officer (E-8), with 16 years of service behind me, and facing combat conditions for the first time. At 36, I had about 3 years of college, been to Japan and Taiwan, studied history and political science, and had a fairly good historical perspective of Vietnam's significance in the world community. I was (to use a Marine Corps phrase, itself borrowed from Chinese) *gung ho.*

So much for the book knowledge. **Then I bounced off Reality**. The Rules of Engagement, the ignored intelligence reports before Tet 68, the *kowtow* (also from the Chinese, meaning "9 bows") obeisance of General Westmoreland to LBJ's ego, all served to shatter an innocence I had kept longer than most. I was senior enough to observe the confusion of the upper brass, old enough to have other realities with which to relate, and still young enough to hurt. *That* was Vietnam.

It's not that I'm older, now. What is really tough is that I was older, then.

1996

WHAT WOULD WE DO WITHOUT JANE FONDA?

In the past, I have written about the educational aspects of the various VVA meetings and conventions I have attended. I talked about the people, the information, and the various fund-raising activities used by the host Vietnam Vets chapters of the events.

So it was with the Region 9 meeting in Carson City I attended last May. At Carson City there was a raffle, an art sale and, perhaps the most interesting, the sales table. I always find these interesting because of the variety of items available - T-shirts, mugs, jackets, unit pins, bumper stickers, and hat or lapel pins. And it occurs to me that the unofficial motto of all those sales tables has to be "Thank God (or, at least, Thank Henry Fonda) for Jane Fonda."

Without that ubiquitous name, Profits from T-shirt sales, lapel pin sales, toilet and urinal sticker sales, and the sale of just about anything else that can hold a meaningful, or meaningless, slogan, would be cut in half, at least.

I have always felt that since people put up with my occasionally unpopular views – the significance of the Peace Movement, young Bill Clinton's opposition to the War, the "America-Love It or Leave It" mindset. etc. – I had better be tolerant of the attitudes of others. In one of the prior issues of this newsletter, I gave my opinion of the phrase," If you weren't there, shut up!" So, to repeat myself: People have been tolerant of my views; I've tried to be tolerant of theirs. But Carson City ended that.

At least in one small aspect. Outside the meeting room, one of the chapters had set up the usual table, selling most of the usual items: T-shirts expressing pride in being a Vietnam Veteran, support for the Wall, support for Harley Davidson, F (whatever) Jane Fonda, unit and area of-duty patches. As I noted, the usual stuff. I own quite a few of these already, so I was looking for something new.

I found it ...and it upset me - totally, deeply, angrily. I cannot now think of it without getting upset. In fact, I cannot now even tell you if it was a T-Shirt or a bumper sticker. It read, "I'll forgive Jane Fonda when the Jews forgive Hitler." And I said to myself, "No. Tolerance has its ending point. Some things are just too far out to be acceptable by even the most easy-going thinking person." And I am not especially easygoing.

I'll forgive Jane Fonda when the Jews forgive Hitler. That comparison is odious, offensive, and obscene. And that just barely gets into the letter "o." The illegitimate, ill-conceived, imbecilic idiot who came up with that thought understands nothing about Vietnam, nothing about Jane Fonda, nothing about the Holocaust and, very probably, nothing about America. Even more probably, nothing about basic arithmetic.

To equate Jane Fonda's protests with the state-directed annihilation of 12 million Jews, Poles, Slavs, Gypsies, homosexuals, and other "undesirables" stuns the imagination. Am I over-reacting? No! There is no way any condemnation could be over-reaction.

The funny thing is, I cannot tell you in an understandable manner why it offends me. It is just so outrageous, so absurd, so ridiculous, so stupid, that my reaction can only be an emotional one.

I could more readily accept that tomorrow's sun would rise in the west, the apple would fly up from the tree, or the earth would start rotating on an equatorial axis, than accept, not the statement, itself, but that someone even close to human, even claiming the rudimentary ability to think, could come up with such a statement.

'Nuff said. I'm out of breath.

1994

This was written as a six-minute speech delivered on April 29, 1979, when I was a member of the Challengers Toastmasters. As a speech, it had been delivered in different forms as far back as 1969. I delivered a version of it in 1970 at a Speech Seminar at the Naval Academy in Annapolis, Maryland. I won my section's competition, and was the first enlisted man ever to be in the finals. So much for that. I didn't win, of course, but I was also the only one totally ignored by the Navy CHINFO (Chief of Information), an Airedale (a Naval Aviation officer, in this case, a rear admiral). This was before CHINFO became a Navy Public Affairs Officer billet. On the other hand, considering my reputation among Navy Public Affairs officers, it wouldn't have made much difference.

One positive thing to come out of that one week seminar was that my section created an award for me, a mounted can of Campbell's soup for a speech in the group in which I said that a good sailor is like chicken soup; some are just saltier than others.

CHOOSING THE PAIN

Several years ago, Barbara Streisand and Robert Redford made a movie about growing up in the 30s and 40s, before and during World War II. The movie ended up in the early 50s, the time of the Korean War. It was a movie of memories, of the way things were.

In the movie Streisand sang of exactly that...the way we were. And in that award-winning song was one particularly perceptive line, one transcending the period of the movie, one which is timeless in its echoing of the human condition: What's too painful to remember, we simply choose to forget. We **choose** to forget. We choose...to forget.

World War II, Korea. Wars we fought. Wars in which we achieved our objectives—the defeat of Germany and Japan in one, the preservation of the integrity of South Korea and containment of North Korea in the other. World War II and the Korean Conflict (as it was known back then).

And then, of course, there was Vietnam, the longest war in our history. It ran, according to Congress (and who would know better) from 1964-1976. Twelve years. Quite a period to forget. If we could. If we wanted to. If we chose to. And for a while, we chose to. We chose to forget.

However, it the last year, we have had a series of movies to remind us. *Coming Home...Heroes...Who'll Stop the Rain...The Deer Hunter...Apocalypse, Now...*and a revival the unforgettable documentary, *Hearts and Minds*. So, maybe we don't want to forget. Maybe we no longer **choose** to forget.

And that, finally, is good. In 1956 Claude G. Bowers wrote, "History is the torch that is meant to illuminate the past, to guard us against the repetition of our mistakes of other days." He was speaking of the Spanish Civil War, but it could have been any war in any history. He was, after all, paraphrasing the earlier twentieth century philosopher, George Santayana, who said "Those who forget their history are condemned to relive it."

Relive it? Relive Vietnam. Relive Que Son, Khontum, the Tet Offensive, *My Lai,* Kent State? Relive the war that brought the mobs into the streets, sent thousands of young Americans into voluntary exile, maimed hundreds of thousands and killed 58,000 more, and sent a president into early retirement, declining to run for another term.

Why would we want to relive it? Merely the thought of that pain makes the pain of remembering almost a blessing.

What was Vietnam? There was no Maine or Pearl Harbor to remember, or the still questionable Tonkin Gulf Incident. *Remember the C. Turner Joy!* It's just not the same. There were no gallant soldiers defending their homeland against foreign invaders, or a Normandy Invasion to inflame the imagination, only a *My Lai* to trouble the conscience.

What was Vietnam? It was a state of mind where American soldiers, sailors and marines, newly arrived in-country, were given a two-day orientation on winning the hearts and minds of the Vietnamese people. It was where they were told that any man, woman or child could be the enemy. I wondered then, silently, that if any man, woman or child could be enemy, who were our friends? Sometimes, it was hard to tell.

What was Vietnam? It was a place where the Saigon Deputy to the National Assembly could ask, during a debate on the draft in 1967, "Why should we send our boys to fight the American's war?"

What was Vietnam? If you believe the peculiar language of the time, it was a war in which no people were killed. Oh, sure, they were greased, or wasted or washed or popped or zapped, but never killed. And they were never people. They were gooks, or slopes, or dinks, or slants. Or, sometimes, friendlies. So you could grease a slope in Vietnam, and talk yourself into thinking you were skiing, not killing. If you believed the words. And we believed the words. We had to believe the words or, at least, hide our thoughts within them. If we didn't, we'd have known we shouldn't have fought, we wouldn't have fought, we couldn't have fought. But we did fight. With guns, and bombs, and napalm, and words.

And now, the movies are here, the words come back, the pain returns. And with it, the way we were. Not how the military dispatches always tell it, though the facts are there, if you know the code, if where the action reports say *fortified bunkers,* you read *houses;* if where the dispatches read *suspected VC sympathizers, you read rice farmers;* if where the official language says *neutralized,* you read *killed!*

And it wasn't the way the movies tell it. Not entirely. It wasn't all drinking and whoring and pot smoking, or Roger Staubach throwing a football at the Seabee base in Da Nang. Or even men killing men and being killed. It was that, but much more. But we know that, if we choose to know that, if we choose to remember.

Can we answer in six minutes questions which will be asked for sixty years, or a hundred and sixty years? Probably not.

But we can choose to remember Rudyard Kipling, writing of another time, another battle, "Almighty God, forgive us yet, lest we forget...lest we forget."

1979

AUTHOR'S NOTE. Now, 33 years later, in 2012, I am forced to ask, "Have the politicians and the generals forgotten? Have they not learned anything? Desert Storm, Iraq, Afghanistan? Are we still choosing to forget?"

This is a speech I gave to a group of Toastmasters in April 1970. It's similar in spots to "Choosing the Pain," in that it expresses my disillusionment with the military near the end of my career. No doubt it contributed to my retirement. It also helped supply the title to the revised form of my first book, "Moveable Forts & Magazines: A Novel of Vietnam," which I renamed "Tarnished Brass Curtain: A Novel of Vietnam." I've supplied the positions (in brackets) held by the several people mentioned.

THE CORROSIVE EFFECTS OF TARNISHED BRASS

"The Military Establishment has terminal cancer, but hasn't the good sense to roll over and die." That statement was made to me over cocktails last summer by a Marine Gunnery Sergeant due to retire shortly.

What made that statement doubly interesting was that he was the epitome of the establishment military man, himself. He was a former Drill Instructor, a veteran of the Korean Conflict, known to those of us who participated in it as WWII-1/2, as well as of the

Vietnam War, known to those who participated in it as futile, frustrating, fouled up, or any other word you care to choose.

That brief comment, amplified as the night wore on, served as a sort of minor revelation. If nothing else, it catalyzed a personal uncertainty that I, also a career military man, has been experiencing. [I was to retire a year later.] He had served in I Corps, the northernmost section of South Vietnam, and had served at Khe Sanh, during the famous siege, while I had served in the Mekong Delta and had been in Saigon during the equally famous Tet Offensive. Two different areas of conflict, two different types of warfare, yet we both had the same feeling of policy confusion and misdirected effort.

He was an infantryman, primarily concerned with the art of war, itself, while I was a public information man, deeply concerned with appearance and image. Both of us considered ourselves patriots and good Americans, yet both were vaguely unhappy.

So, I sat down and looked at the situation. I looked at military events for only the past year, beginning with my involvement with the USS Pueblo hearings Command Information Bureau. What I discovered was extremely interesting, though disturbing. Or extremely disturbing, though interesting. Somewhere between policy creation and policy execution, somewhere between the minor gods who make the decisions and we groundlings who carry them out, there is a short circuit.

A third group has interposed itself. This group can be represented by a token figure, a symbolic personification of what is wrong with the military today. His uniform could be blue, white, green or Khaki, but his emblem best describes him. For the sake of identification, we'll call him the man in tarnished brass.

There are many examples of his influence but, considered en masse, I get confused. As a Master Chief Petty Officer with 18 years in the the Navy, I realize I am part of the Establishment. Therefore, I cannot attack, I cannot engage in polemics, I can only appraise.

1969 opened with the USS Pueblo Court of Inquiry. Remember the Pueblo? What did we discover? Confusion, contradicting order, lack of a positive policy. The military image was dimmed. I, a career petty officer, was less a man.

The EC-121 spy plane that was shot down over North Korean waters, even as the Pueblo inquiry was in progress, proved how little we had learned. But those incidents presented only a part of the picture, one direction from which the military has damaged itself.

There was, of course, General Turner [Provost-General of the Army, who had been accused of selling Army weapons] and his second hand gun shop. A nice setup for the Army's head policeman. No summary of moral decay would be complete with a mention of the Sergeant Major Woolridge [senor army enlisted man, accused of skimming slot machine profits in Vietnam] Incentive Awards Program.

The damage these two men have done to all career military men will not be fully assessed for years. And so the Brass was tarnished even more.

Brass tarnished green which brings up Col. Rheult and his gang of Green Berets. {Here, I confess, I don't remember the exact incident, other than it made the news.] Did they or did they not terminate the alleged victim with extreme prejudice? The Green Berets weren't saying and the Army wasn't saying. Funny, neither was the CIA. Except it wasn't funny.

As 1969 came to a close, the Man in Tarnished Brass was revealed as having worked on his newest project, an untidy 1968 little drama in 109 acts entitled "The My Lai Massacre." Here we saw a captain, some lieutenants and a handful of enlisted men being indicted on assorted crimes of murder, rape and other personal indignities.

And the tarnish has crept upward. Fourteen more Army officers, two of them generals, have been added to the list.

The tragedy of My Lai has added a new phrase to our history, as well as a black pun. Me Lie! How singularly, frighteningly, sickeningly appropriate. How much I and my Marine friend, career military men both, would like to stare this man in tarnished brass in his tarnished collective eye and say, "Yes, you lie. And continue to do so. To us, our fellow career men, to the men who work with us and for us. You have blackened our image, compromised our reputation and made us sick and ashamed." Yet, in retrospect, saying this would mean very little. He wouldn't care.

It would probably be nice—probably—if, after cataloguing this list of moral aggressions against the American Dream, I could offer you a solution to the problem. I cannot.

All I can offer you is a view of some Pueblo vacillation, high level greed, Green Beret mystery, USS Evans confusion, some C5A fiscal manipulation [here I admit to not remembering what these last two incident were, other than they were in the news at the time] and stir gently with a ten-foot pole.

If you come up with the same mélange of military mis-management I have, you'll understand why so many career military men are thoughtfully, calculatedly, and with regret, crying, "We want out!"

April 1970

This was written in December 1993, with references to Somalia, Bosnia, and Operation Desert Storm. To those, we can possibly add Iraq and Afghanistan. Eighteen years later, the question remains relevant.

IS THE VIETNAM WAR IRRELEVANT?
Has the Vietnam War Been Forgotten?

The first reaction is to say, "Of course, not. No way? Can't happen!" That's the first reaction. But after that, after the surprise, after the shock, the question repeats itself: Has the Vietnam been forgotten?

It's a valid question. Has it been forgotten as a war? Has it been forgotten as a personal experience? It hasn't been—not by us, not by the guys who served and hurt and survived there. It never will be.

But what about as a National Experience? Has it become a symbol, a cliché to be used by politicians? "Somalia must never become another Vietnam." "As we become involved in Bosnia, the Vietnam Syndrome clicks in."

As a symbol of national conscience, it remains. Much as the Korean Conflict (never officially a war) became "The Forgotten War," however, Vietnam can be relegated to *phrase status.*

For years we were forgotten, ignored, written off. Then, during *Operation Desert Storm,* we were suddenly discovered, for a moment; honored, for a moment; given a part in the Hollywood Parade honoring those who followed us, for a moment; remembered in a few movies; for a moment; and then, forgotten again, dismissed from the national awareness.

Twenty years ago, in the movie, *The Way We Were,* Barbara Streisand sang, "What's too painful to remember, we simply choose to forget." That may have become the theme song of the generations other than ours. "It was too painful, it didn't make sense. We don't understand it. Let's forget it."

So, they can forget it. *They* can. We can't. **Do we really want to?**

You're History!!!

If you watched the movies of the 80's, or re-watched them on TV, you'll recognize the headline phrase — YOU'RE HISTORY! It was generally uttered by a gangster-type with a snarl and a Magnum .44.

It meant, depending upon your frame of reference, you *are about to be dead... you are about to be gone from the scene... out of someone's life,* etc.

However, I was recently introduced to a new meaning to the phrase. This happened when I was speaking with Ben Arguello, the 9th grade history teacher at Pacoima Middle School.

Ben had asked for Chapter 419's help in providing Vietnam vets for his students to interview. He said he wanted to get his students to view history as being alive, as being something other than the dead past.

So, we provided some members to be interviewed. Even I was interviewed. I answered questions concerning my feelings about the war, about being sent, what I ate, whether I killed anyone, and other questions connected with my experiences.

Throughout it all, my underlying thought was that I represented to these kids what a World War I vet represented to me — someone who participated in a war that ended long before I was born. Was I up to being history? The students were reading about the war in their books; the book reading was supplemented by Ben Arguello's lecture; the action was personalized by me, a participant. I was making history come alive; I was history. The things they read about — Saigon, the Tet Offensive, the Mekong Delta, the news reporters and their cameras, the Caravelle Hotel (I doubt if they read anything about the Caravelle, but it was part of *my* history) — all these things had been a part of my life.

There was an urge to pontificate, to exaggerate my feelings, or denigrate them. I didn't know how to answer some of the questions. After all, I was history! Did I want to be? I had no choice. It was all in the past. And the past can be discussed, regretted, remembered, glorified, denied, ignored; but it cannot be changed.

So, I stopped trying to figure out what I wanted to say, stopped trying to figure out what the students wanted to hear, stopped trying to second-guess everything., and just started to answer the questions as honestly as I could. I decided to let the students put their own interpretations on what they heard.

I didn't have to do anything special. I had already done that. After all, I was history.

March 1995

I wrote this in 1995, shortly after the book came out. It was later printed in the VVA

California state newspaper, "California Zephyr," of which I was a contributing writer. My hope is that our current military leaders have read McNamara's 11 points and have adopted them and adapted. At the time I write this, in summer, 2012, I am not totally convinced they have done so.

MacNAMARA'S "REVELATION" REVEALS LITTLE

A REVIEW BY DICK ROSE

<u>IN RETROSPECT: THE TRAGEDIES AND LESSONS OF VIETNAM</u>
by **Robert S. McNamara** *with Brian VanDeMark*, **Times Books, Random House,** ©**1995**

McNamara has written a book, and everyone seems upset. The simplest summary would be this: We screwed up!

And that is the message that has so many vets upset. As if they hadn't known. I knew from the moment in 1968, in Saigon, when I attended a MAC-V briefing for Admiral Kenneth Veth, Commander, Naval Forces, Vietnam.

"Admiral," the Army intelligence captain said, "LBJ doesn't want to hear bad news, and therefore, General Westmoreland does not want to hear bad news."

Forget the rules of engagement, the sanctuaries across the border, the bombing cessations – that nameless captain's statement was *the* policy statement of the war from 1968 on, whatever it might have been before then.

The key statement in McNamara's book occurs in Chapter One, on page four, when McNamara is giving a little personal background that has **nothing** to do with the war. He describes entering school in 1922, noting that the school was a wooden shack, the accommodations were poor, but the teacher was excellent.

"At the end of the month she gave us a test and reassigned our seating based on the results; the student with the highest grade would sit in the front seat in the leftmost row.

"I was determined to occupy that seat. The class was predominantly WASP – white Anglo-Saxon Protestants – but my competitors for the top spot were invariably Chinese, Japanese, and Jews. After each week of hard work, I would spend Saturday and Sunday playing with my neighborhood friends while my rivals went to ethnic schools, studied their ancestral languages, absorbed ancient and complex cultures, and returned to school on Monday determined to beat their Irish classmate. I am happy to say they rarely did."

And there it is, the quintessential McNamara – the acorn boy who became the oak Secretary of Defense – the spark plug that drove the Ford industrial giant. This throw-away anecdote both supports and undercuts everything that is to follow in this 346 page (not including 46 pages of footnotes and acknowledgments and 11 pages *of personae)* book.

The early blooming arrogance of the driven achiever – playing on the weekend, yet outdoing his hard-studying schoolmates – is a foreshadowing of the man who was to be the leader of "the best and the brightest." He refers to the group in his Preface:

"My associates in the Kennedy and Johnson administrations were an exceptional group: young, vigorous, intelligent, well-meaning, patriotic servants of the United States. How did the group – 'the best and the brightest,' as we eventually came to be known in an ironically pejorative phrase – get it wrong on Vietnam?"

He calls it "ironically pejorative," yet he never seems to relinquish his right to use the phrase – with pride – to describe himself.

He condenses his World War II service years discussing how he started out teaching modem statistical controls to the US 8th Air Force and ended the war as a Lieutenant Colonel stricken with polio.

He then joined the legendary "Tex" Thornton at Ford. 'Because of our cerebral approach to making decisions and our youth, "he writes, "we became known as the 'Whiz Kids.'" "We" being the group of young executives that rose with him, an early version of "the best and the brightest." Fifteen years later, he was president of the company.

The War

There is little he says that should be news to anyone. Nevertheless, his saying it removes our last vestiges of innocence and self-delusion. Up to now, we (in the military) may have realized we were whores, but we could kid ourselves that we retained – in some mysterious way – our virginity. The war was wrong for any number of reasons, we felt, but somehow, we could still retain some feeling that what we did – in some enigmatic way – was right.

This book shatters all those illusions of purity of purpose. It strips us of our last vestiges of virginity. It shows that the war was fought as a political exercise, not a moral one. The goals were ill-defined, the enemy was underestimated, our allies were overrated, the battles reduced to mere statistics, and the troops seen as mere barter points. We were used, as savagely, as brutally, as callously, as any "Saigon Tea" girl in a *Tu Do* Street bar.

McNamara makes a lot of points in this book, quotes a lot of statistics, gives a lot of facts, and makes one gigantic leap of faith based on John F. Kennedy's statements to his advisors during the Cuban Missile Crisis, "that the United States must make every effort to avoid the risk of an unpredictable war.?"

"So I conclude that John Kennedy would have eventually gotten out of Vietnam rather than move more deeply in. I express this judgment now because, in light of it, I must explain how we -including Lyndon Johnson – who continued in policy-making roles after President Kennedy's death made the decisions leading the eventual deployment to Vietnam of half a million U.S. combat troops. Why did we do what we did, and what lessons can *be* learned from our actions?"

It takes another 223 pages – including pictures – for McNamara to answer his own question. But in the process, he does identify what factors led to the disaster – eleven of them, in fact, which he summarizes for us:

1. "We misjudged, and continued to do so, the intentions of North Vietnam and the Viet Cong and exaggerated their danger to the United States.

2. We viewed the leaders and people of South Vietnam by our own standards, assuming a drive for democracy stronger than it was and ignoring the internal political situation.

3. We underestimated the power that `Nationalism" has to motivate the North Vietnamese and Viet Cong to fight and die for their beliefs and values.

4. We misjudged friend and foe alike because of our profound ignorance of the history, culture, and politics of the people, and the personalities and habits of their leaders.

5. We failed to recognize the limitations of our hi-tech military equipment, <u>failing,</u> too, to adapt our military tactics to win the hearts and minds of people from a totally different culture.

6. We failed to include the public – including their elected officials – in the decision-making process before becoming involved in a large-scale military action.

7. After we got involved, we failed to explain what was happening, why we did what we did, and, thus, did not get popular support at home for our actions.

8. We did not recognize that "[w]e do not have the God-given right to shape every nation in our image "

9. We didn't hold to the principle that, except for direct threats to our national security, we should only act in multi-national efforts.

10. We failed to recognize that in international affairs, there may be problems for which there are no immediate solutions.

11. Underlying most of these was that we failed to adequately analyze the enormous costs – in time, materiel, and most importantly, human lives – and to properly define the nebulous benefits of the war.

The lesson he derives from all the mistakes we made and the tremendous price we paid is a noble one, one which he admits he doesn't know how to apply:

"In sum, we should strive to create a world in which relations among nations would be based on the rule of law, a world in which national security would be supported by a system of collective security. The conflict prevention, conflict resolution, and peace-keeping functions necessary to accomplish these objectives would be performed by multilateral institutions, a reorganized and strengthened United Nations together with new and expanded regional organizations.

"That is my vision of the post-Cold War world. In the post-Cold War world, the United States should *be* clear about where, and how, it would apply military force. This requires a precise statement of U. S. Foreign policy objectives..

"The Unites States clearly cannot and should not intervene in every conflict arising from a nation's attempts to move toward capitalist democracy. .Nor can we be expected to try to stop by military force every instance of the slaughter of innocent civilians."

The Book

The summary, while helpful, is in no way equal to the parts. Regardless of your involvement in the war or your views on it, *you* – whoever you are – should read this book. Forget about the possible $15 or $20 in McNamara's pocket; what he gives you is full value.

The book has something for everyone: the former protester at Berkeley or Lincoln Park or London; the draft eligible young man who sought sanctuary in Canada; the "Nuke 'em to Hell" cold warrior; the bruised soldier; or the untouched modern historian.

McNamara presents a finely detailed picture of good intentions gone awry, leading to unavoidable disaster and needless suffering. He shows us that good intentions cannot overcome arrogance, innocence, incompetence, abstinence, intransigence, and an overwhelming need for self-deception.

If LBJ did not want to hear bad news, and General Westmoreland did not want to hear bad news, Robert S. McNamara and his band of "the best and the brightest" did not try hard enough to force the bad news upon them. Though he doesn't say so, McNamara lacked the courage to tell the truth when the truth was painful to say and painful to hear. Nor did he adopt the policy – that so many junior officials did – that to be true to oneself and to one's beliefs are more important than the job. He didn't push, he didn't resign. What he did do, what he admits to doing – but not in those words – was to commit himself to the lowest level of legislative-bureaucratic ethics. He went along to get along.

He just couldn't give up that front seat in the leftmost row.

POETRY

No book about being in Vietnam would be complete without including a bit of doggerel, ubiquitous poems that seemed to crop up everywhere. Most were scatological, but that wasn't my style.

I'm including only those that I wrote. Some rhyme, some scan, most don't.

Nevertheless, for your entertainment, I offer the following pages. I included "Interview With a Sergeant," earlier. That was serious. For the most part, these aren't.

August 2012

Flying High With Semper Fi

One of the perks of being the Senior Chief at Naval Forces, VN, headquarters Public Affairs Office, was that I could choose my own forays into the field.

Among the most memorable was the time I spent in March, 1968, at Nha Be with Marine Advisory Team (MAT) 43. They were training the Xung Kich, a group of Vietnamese commandos, all volunteers, who, ultimately, were so good that they showed up the ARVN Regular Forces, and were disbanded.

I joined them on a midnight ambush op, and still remember sitting there, watching the grenade and claymore explosions, the tracers from the Hueys which came to our defense, and the M-16s and AK-47s trading bullets, and thinking: This is a hell of a place for a Jewish boy on St. Patrick's Day.

I also remember the camaraderie of Captains Dunning and Brown, Sergeants Sam Garland and James May, HM1 "Doc" Ledue, and their Vietnamese commandos, and how they accepted me, even giving me a Marine boonie hat. To immortalize the experience, I wrote the following poem for them, the day I left Nha Be to return to Saigon.

Flying High with Semper Fi

Tiger suit in shades of green
Floppy bush hat never clean
Great in strength and bright of eye
You're looking at a "Semper Fi."
 When the road starts getting rougher
 Our bright-eyed hero starts getting tougher.
 "The enemy's ahead," he yells to the sky.
 "And don't forget, we're 'Semper Fi.' "
"Quit your yelling, you stupid jerk,
Or this ambush op will never work."
The sergeant grunts, with steel in his eye
"There's a time and a place for 'Semper Fi'
 "I admire your nerve, I admire your guts,
 But yelling on ambush is strictly for nuts.
 Now is the time for peace and for quiet,
 It's a hell of a place to 'Semper Fi' it.
"You're a Marine, inside you know it.
It's through your actions that you'll show it.
When the dolls begin to give you the eye,
That's the time to slip in your 'Semper Fi.' "

 Now, from this swabbie, all kidding aside.
 I salute your motto, in which you take pride.
May the fame of your name, grow wider and higher
And may they never extinguish your Semper Fire.

1968

The Vietnam War was traumatic; but there were some lighter moments, especially if you were an REMF (Rear Echelon M-F) stationed in Saigon before Tet. To get from place to place, you had to rely on the MAC-V bus line run by US Army Headquarters Area Command (USAHAC — pronounced you-sa-hack), which connected the various exchanges, BOQs, BEQs, mess halls, and Command Headquarters.

I wrote this in late '67. Contraband copies ended up being posted by unknown admirers at — where else — MAC-V bus stops–those ubiquitous cornerssurrounded by cement-filled 55-gallon drums.

Waiting For a MAC-V Bus
(or)
How I Spent My First Year
Behind the Barrel

An epic ballad, composed on the spot, and in agony extremis, by the Mad (and angry, even) Balladeer of Saigon City.

When the sun was high and it was time for Lunch,
I left my office, some chow to munch.
Behind the barrels, some five of us
Awaitin' for the MAC-V bus.

Two buses to catch and my meal to devour –
I had said I'd return in about an hour,

I was new in-country, a naive young cuss
Who'd never waited for a MAC-V bus.

Twelve minutes later, we were still waiting.,
But 'twas not yet too aggravating,
'Cause we knew before the wait got too arduous
We'd be riding a jolly MAC-V bus.

Still we were waiting, an hour later,
Our anxiety was growing greater.
By now a crowd, 35 of us
Were waiting for the MAC-V bus.

Three hours later, 'twas not so fine,
Fifteen lay wounded by a Claymore mine,.
The VC loves crowds so numerous
Waiting for a MAC-V bus.

As darkness fell, an Old Timer said,
Noticing blood dripping down my head,
"Orange line or Blue, Cofat or Brinks,
The whole transportation system stinks.
As the night goes on, your determination
Will only get you a curfew violation.
You may rant and rave and scream and cuss,
But you'll never catch a MAC-V bus!"

But as the moon started rising higher
An apparition appeared, wreathed in fire,
"Caesar I am, famed Julius,
Watching you wait for a MAC-V bus.
I was stabbed in the Forum I suppose they told you.
'Twas just a story Shakespeare sold you.
When Brutus done me in, 'twas more treacherous,
He made me wait for a MAC-V bus."

And, suddenly, 'twas as I feared,
Other historical persons appeared,
Telling their tales so wondrous.
Each had waited for a MAC-V bus,

Napoleon and Nero, Marie Antoinette –
All had waited and none could forget.
But de Sade, at his worst, would never discuss
What it's like to wait for a MAC-V bus.

Yet, after I'd waited another hour
I realized not even Flower Power
Could smite the might of the fatuous
Jerk who scheduled the MAC-V bus.

The Old Timer, still with saddened eye,
Said, "You're wasting your time, and I'll tell you why.
The buses are run by USAHAC, see?
So you might as well take a 50 P taxi.

You're a new man, I see, in Saigon fair.
Listen! And learn, to your despair,
The truth. So simple, it's ridiculous.
There's no such thing as a MAC-V bus!"

(L'Envoi)
That's the end of the story I've had to relate.
In poetry, the tale I more easily state,
But the author remains anonymous,
Fearing the vengeance a mythical bus.
 (c'est finis)

Fall, 1967 ©1995

Marvin the ARVN

It didn't take me long in Vietnam before I learned of the reputation of the Army of the Republic of Vietnam (The ARVN). They were not admired (if I may put it mildly.) Perhaps, in retrospect, I may have done them a misservice, but this was almost forty years ago, on the spot, as it were.)

There once was a young man named Marvin,
Who was drafted into the ARVN.
    He was given some arms
    And sent to the farms
To keep the poor peasants from starvin'.

But they were fatter before Marvin got there,
Tending their rice and their plot there.
    He was stealing their chickens,
    While GIs caught the dickens,
Ensuring that Charlie was not there.

So Marvin soldiered by day, but not night,
Kept his mess hall always in sight.
    Said he, "It's too hot!

Let the Americans get shot.
Besides, it's not really my fight."

One day he went out to make war.
Till his feet start getting too sore.
    Before he went far, he
    Went over to Charlie,
Now Marvin's an ARVN no more.

Now this may sound bitter, 'tis true.
But I want to get just one thought through.
    Don't worry 'bout Marvin,
    The non-fighting ARVN;
It's not him you're protecting, it's you.

November, 1967

November, 1967, two months after I arrived in country, I was down in one of the largest towns in the Mekong Delta, Vinh Long, doing a story on the PBR sailors, and the helicopter unit, with a side trip to a Seabee outfit. I had hitched a ride from the airbase to the Navy base, and when the Seabee found out what I was there for, he suggested I write up his unit. I did. It was called "The Peace Corps of the Navy."

However, after a mission with the helicopter unit, most of the enlisted men gathered at what they called "The Ol' Swimming Hole, a large pit dug for them by the Seabees, filled with water and using a old helicopter blade for a diving board, although few dove, given the shallow water. I joined them. I cannot say it was refreshing, since the water was warm and muddy, and not much relief from the mugginess of the jungle area.

One of the sailors had a guitar and started singing western songs. Then they started with a few spontaneous additions in the style of what I assume was a southern tradition around a campfire. After everyone who wanted to had contributed, someone said, "Hey, Chief, you're a writer, why don't you sing something. So, out of the air, aided by a beer I had been drinking, I joined in. It wasn't quite out of the air, since it had been brewing in my head, along with the beer, while they were all singing their ditties.

Oh, once I had plenty of money,
Which I lavished on my brown-eyed honey.
I ran out cash and
She ran out of passion,
And somehow the ending ain't funny

And now I come to the Christmas song parodies. It was close to Christmas, 1967, when one of our Journalists, Tom Walton, JO1 (Journalist First Class), said, "Hey, guys, listen to this. He then proceded to read an action report from one of the HA(L) Three (Helicopter Attack Squadron 3) the Seawolves, pilots. I don't remember the exact numbers, but it was something like '...three fortified bunkers, two VC fishnets, three VC sampans...' and someone yelled out 'and a partridge in a pear tree,' to which I responded, "No, a sniper in a palm tree'" and that set us off to writing "The Saigon Songbook for a Cool Yule," by Sailor No-man and the Anonymice.

It was a slow day and we had already completed our report for the news media at the "Five O'clock Follies," held, of course at 6:00 pm. So, we all started writing with increased enthusiasm. I include here only those I actually wrote.

SEAWOLF PACIFICATION
(Deck the Halls)

Shoot them up with Willy Peter (white phosphorous), Fa la la
la la, la la la lah;
Interdiction couldn't be neater, Fa la la la la, la la la lah.
Grab M-60, load the rockets, Fa la la la la, la la la lah;
We kill VC, so don't knock it, Fa la la la la, la la la lah.

(Note: NAVFOR-V is the Naval Forces Vietnam Command)

NAVFOR-V
(Jingle Bells)

NavFor-V, NavFor-V, NavFor-V's our home,
Here we sit at NavFor-V, nevermore to roam. (Repeat)

A week or two ago, we thought we'd take a trip,
The admiral said, "No, because you're not a VIP."
But still we thought we'd try, the fight force to see;
We figured out how we could fly, we'd fly on LSD!

NavFor-V, NavFor-V, NavFor-V's our home,
Here we sit at NavFor-V, nevermore to roam. (Repeat)

Richard S. Rose

(MAC O-I was the Military Assistance Command (General Westmore-land) Office of Information. Everything we wrote had to go through that office before it could be released.)

OH, MAC O-I
(Oh, Christmas Tree (or) O, Tannenbaum)

Oh, MAC O-I, Oh, MAC O-I,
How funny are your rules and regs. (Repeat)

We say, "capture," you say detain,
We ask you why, you don't explain.
Oh, MAC O-I, Oh, MAC O-I,
How funny are your rules and regs.

The "hooches we shot yesterday,
Are "bunkers" now, or so you say.
Oh, MAC O-I, Oh, MAC O-I,
How funny are your rules and regs.

OH, VIETNAM
(Oh, MAC-OI)

Oh, Vietnam, Oh, Vietnam
How funny are your residents.

Oh, Vietnam, Oh, Vietnam
How funny are your residents.

You invite us in to fight your war,
Take all our cash, and ask for more.
Oh, Vietnam, Oh, Vietnam
How funny are your residents.

Oh, Vietnam, Oh, Vietnam
How funny are your residents.
They eat fish and *nuoc mam**, washed down with beer,
Then wonder why we don't come near.
Oh, Vietnam, Oh, Vietnam
How funny are your residents.
*Nuoc Mam is odorous, very spicy fermented fish oil

Oh, Vietnam, Oh, Vietnam
How funny are your residents.
We train your troops, and make them strong,
And then they join the Viet Cong.
Oh, Vietnam, Oh, Vietnam
How funny are your residents.

———————————————

(And now my favorite—first because of its inherent bitter ending, and second because if I had realized exactly what I was writing, I couldn't have written it. A PBR is a 31-foot fiberglass, heavily armed, lightly armored, water-jet driven boat, Go watch "Apocalypse Now" for visual details.)

WE'RE CRUISING DOWN THE MEKONG RIVER

(White Christmas)

> We're cruising down the Mekong River,
> In our old leaky P-B-R,
> Where the palm trees rustle and VC hustle
> To see that we don't get too far.
> We're cruising down the Mekong River,
> Shooting at the enemy we see.
> May the river always remain free
> And may all our victims be VC.

(And so we had a jolly, pre-TET Offensive holiday time.

FICTION

This is a chapter from my novel, "Tarnished Brass Curtain: A Novel of Vietnam." I've included it in this book because I lived it. Fred is a fictional character, but if you substitute me, his feelings were mine, and the satchel charge and mortar attack were real. In fact, the whole situation was real. I was assigned to HA(L)3, Detachment 3, to write a story about them.

The novel was written in 1975 as my Master's Thesis and to rid me of my demons. I've compressed some of the opinions and conversations I heard at various times into one time period.

AND ON THE SEVENTH DAY

April in Vietnam is hot. In the Mekong Delta, it is hot and relatively dry. The summer monsoon rains have not yet come to raise the river, flooding the few roads that exist in that aqueous world. No, in April, the roads still connect the major cities of the Delta.

The five fingers of the Mekong River reach out from the wrist near Tan Chau, close to the Cambodian border. They have many names–My Tho, Ham Luong, Co Chien, the Bassac, and several others. They flow on, reaching out to the South China Sea. There, they are known collectively as the Mouths of the Mekong.

But whether mouths or fingertips, the rivers of the Delta are its lifelines. On them depends most of the commerce on this intricate weave of canals, smaller rivers, and even smaller streams, some barely navigable, but still necessary to the residents of the hamlets, villages and larger towns. On these waterways travel tiny sampans, larger sampans and still larger junks. These vessels carry grain, animals, cloth, vegetables, and people.

But in the early spring of 1968, some of the vessels carried medicine, guns, ammunition, grenades, rocket launchers and Viet Cong, the last being patriots, nationalists, terrorists, or oppressors, depending upon who you were, and what position you occupied in the Delta.

The Mekong Delta, fertile rice bowl of the southern quarter of the Republic of Vietnam, was a much desired piece of real estate. Small names with big meanings dotted the area–Can Tho, My Tho, Sa Dec, Ben Tre, Dong Tam, Vinh Long. The meanings were big to those who had been there. To others they were merely dots on a map, if anyone bothered to look at the map. Few people did.

Another name was Long Duc, an insignificant town on one of the smaller branches. It was a full-fledged town, complete with concrete roads, a decent sanitation system, and a shining new city hall, all courtesy of the U.S. Navy's Peace Corps, the Seabees.

But more than just Seabees were there. River Patrol Boats and attack helicopters were there to keep all of the traffic moving, free from harassment by the Viet Cong, free to carry supplies and food and people.

Lieutenant (junior grade) Alfred (Fred) Thayer Hetherington, Jr., USN, son, grandson, and nephew of numerous admirals and generals, was there, preparing for his first combat mission. At least, he hoped it would be a combat mission, as he had hoped before. He had not yet been blooded, and he had been there six days, already. Thirteen missions and no contact. Maybe this would be lucky fourteen.

He was in the co-pilot seat of-a "Huey," an HU-1B Army attack helicopter, modified for Navy use. The chopper had been checked out, the body examined for any bullet holes and rusty spots, the externally-mounted flex M-60 machine guns lubricated and cleaned of the ever present sand, the rotors examined for anything that might go wrong.

The morning patrol was to be over a VC-controlled area off the Co Chien River, about 20 miles southeast of Long Duc.

Some unusual activity had been reported, and Fred was hoping for action. He looked toward the pilot, Pete Rogers, who started the main rotor, keeping it under the 66-hundred revolutions per minute required to get the craft aloft.

Outside, the maintenance crew members took refuge from the sand blast behind jeeps and maintenance buildings, behind anything that might protect them from the sandstorm being kicked up by River Ranger 51, the lead chopper, skippered by Lt. Commander Sam Silverman, the commander of Detachment 5, Helicopter (Light) Attack Squadron 5, and co-piloted by Lt. (j.g.) Howie Martinez, four months in-country, and a combat veteran.

As 51 lifted off, Rogers received the thumbs-up signal from the maintenance chief, doing double duty as traffic controller, as usual.

Both choppers circled quickly over *Long Duc,* then headed southeast, about to begin a 4 hour reconnaissance mission over the VC-occupied territory on the northeast bank of the river.

"Strictly routine, Fred. But keep an eye out. For the River Rangers, routine means we expect the unexpected." Pete had been in-country 17 months, and was one of the original 32 Navy pilots who had arrived in Vietnam between June and December of 1966, to study for three months under Army pilots, learning combat tactics and gaining familiarity with the "Huey" although he was already a skilled fixed wing and helicopter pilot.

Fred looked at the stocky redhead, the tip of his always peeling nose jutting above his grin, half hidden by the helmet. He found it difficult to believe that Pete had over 800 hours in the "Hueys," earned the Distinguished Flying Cross and Purple Heart while serving with the Army, and an additional Distinguished Flying Cross with the Navy.

Fred, also a trained pilot, had been given 15 hours of aircraft familiarization at Fort Benning, Georgia, and was receiving his in-country training from Pete.

Behind them were Clay Burman and Jack Sierocki, crew chief and right door gunner, respectively. Fred already knew that they were sitting by their doors, relaxed and wary, combat experienced. They should be sitting at home, somewhere, drinking milkshakes, he thought. But they were combat veterans, though younger than he. He looked below him at the jungle, already familiar and unchanging in its vastness, beauty and remoteness.

"River Ranger 51." Fred jerked as the crackling radio voice called the lead ship, identified itself, and mentioned a set of six digit coordinates.

Pete spoke into his mike. "Fred, you're in luck. We've got some action. That was the Ben Tra sector advisor, Sounds like Charlie's active, again."

Hetherington nodded, a movement barely noticeable because of the constant tremor of the chopper vibration. "I figured that. They've got a VN Army unit under fire. Will the ARVN fight?"

Pete laughed. "Hey, Buddy, who've you been talking to? Sure, they'll fight. That's a good outfit around *Ben Tra.* You've been hearing scuttlebutt about the Ninth Division 'Chicken Stealers,' huh?"

The younger pilot turned to look at his aircraft commander, mentor and friend (who, being the pilot, continued to look ahead and all around). "Scuttlebutt? It's not true?"

Rogers laughed again. "Hell, yes, it's true. It's all politics. If they have a gung-ho leader or sector commander, they'll fight. Otherwise, they sort of crawl away when the fighting gets rough. As for the outpost under fire, they're a good crowd. The sector commander isn't on the take or on the make. He's unusual, I agree. But it's not our place to think about politics. Just about Charlie. And he's apparently down there somewhere. Or everywhere." With his left hand he gestured toward the open door, and then tilted the chopper slightly to the left so that Hetherington could see more clearly the area below. Fred was already getting used to the fact the chopper had no doors, and he didn't shrink back quite as much as he had before. He looked down at the grayish green islands of Nipa Palm, bamboo, occasional rice paddies, and a web of small lines radiating from, entwining with, and crossing the main river.

"Mr. Rogers, sir?" Clay Burman's voice came over the ship's intercom, "Maybe he'd like to read 'Marvin the ARVN.'"

"Christ," the pilot's voice returned, "Is that crap still floating around."

"What's that?" Fred's voice sounded interested, even through the electronic filter.

"Just some anonymous doggerel, courtesy of the intellectual desk jockeys at Navy headquarters in Saigon. It's better than most, if not as raunchy. You know, Fred, some guys collect skin books, others cigarette lighters. 'Cincinnati' Clay collects anonymous poetry. I think he's going to put them together in a book or something. How about it, Kid?" He lifted his hand, keeping his eyes on his instrument panel and on the jungle below. "I think he writes it, himself."

"Hey, that's not true, Mr., R. I just find it interesting. Some of it's pretty funny. Especially the 'Twelve Days of Action' takeoff on the 'Twelve Days of Christmas.'"

"Hell, they're all funny. They'd be subversive, too, if they weren't so true. Only, don't let Mr. Hetherington see it, yet. He's still a virgin. Besides his Dad's an *Admiral*."

Fred listened to this interchange with interest. The camaraderie there between the plane commander and his enlisted crew was quite surprising. It didn't fit in with what he had learned about the barrier between the ranks. Still, under these circumstances, such familiarity was relaxing. And he hadn't seen any breach of discipline or low morale in the week he'd been there. Or six days. Today was the seventh. He decided to join in. "I won't tell Dad, I promise."

Pete gave him a "thumbs up" signal, and then pointed forward and to their left. Fred looked, picked up the binoculars to the right of his feet, looked down, and saw nothing. "What am I supposed to be looking at?"

"That's *Ben Tra* over there. There should be some sign of action."

The radio crackled again; Rogers reached over and flipped the earphones from inter-com to radio. Sam Silverman, ahead of them, was calling. "River Ranger 53. Do you see anything?"

Pete's reply was terse. "Negative sighting."

"Ditto. I'll call the ground forces advisor. Let's scout around. You go in first; I'll cover."

"Roger. Down and away!!!" The craft suddenly lurched, the nose headed down, and the <u>whump-whump</u> of the blades was louder as they chewed at the decreased air pressure. Fred watched the altimeter dropping steadily from the 2,000 feet at which they had been cruising.

At 1200 feet Rogers gestured back. "Sam'll stay up here and cover us. Remember, only one member of the team goes in at any one time."

They dropped quickly to 100 feet, where the trees were rushing by them. "Clay! Jack! Take a good look." The two gunners, M-60's cradled and ready in their arms, looked out through the door openings. Pete turned momentarily back toward Fred. "Remember about altitudes, Fred. Either over a thousand, or under a hundred. At 1200 feet, you're too small a target for a rifleman, and at 100 you're too fast a target. Anywhere in between is no-man's land." A pause. "See anything, guys?"

"No sir," came both voices, almost simultaneously.

"Okay. Let's up. Fifty-one'll want to check the area across the river." The chopper rose, approached the lead ship and hovered. Sam Silverman threw an exaggerated salute at his cover man, then dropped his craft, moving along the other side of the river as Pete Rogers had predicted.

For the next thirty minutes, they continued the routine. Fred was sure this would be another mission like all the others. And he'd already been there a week.

He was distracted from his ruminations by a slight sound just to his right, as though a small pebble had hit the frame of the air-craft. "What was..." he began.

"Hostiles," Sierocki yelled, flipping a smoke grenade out his door. The craft rose quickly, Rogers calling his skipper.

"Fifty-One. Have received hostile fire. Going in to investigate."

"Roger, Fifty-three. Return fire, if necessary. We'll cover."

"What about getting permission to return fire?" Fred yelled over the intercom. "Don't the Rules of Engagement require that? In case there are friendlies in the area?"

"Ah, yes, 'The Rules.' You learn fast. Now forget 'em. Sam'll get permission for us." Pete laughed again, then returned his atten-tion to the situation at hand. "Keep an eye on the area of smoke grenade. Clay, I'll throw two rockets, then keep it right. You spray the trees with M-60."

The chopper suddenly plunged down and forward as Rogers executed the maneuver he had just described. Fred's stomach jumped; a strange taste was in his throat; his heart began to beat violently; and an acrid smell assailed his nostrils.

An air of exhilaration overcame him as the adrenalin, cord-ite and centrifugal force worked their spell on him. They passed quickly over the area, then rose and swung around, River Ranger 51 executing a similar maneuver below them.

"Okay, guys," Pete said. "We'll try the same thing on the right. How's your trigger finger, Fred? Want to give it a try?"

"Hell, yes," he yelled, his lungs pumping in swift gasps. His right hand reached for the trigger, prepared to fire the flex-mounted external M-60's. They went in, Fred firing the flex-guns in short bursts ahead of him. He was conscious of Sierocki firing out of the door opening behind him. Time seemed to stop.

"Hey, Fred," Pete called, "Ease up. We've passed the area. They're on our right."

It was Fred's turn to let loose a short laugh, relaxing his hand, and collapsing within himself, suddenly aware of being covered with sweat. His heart gradually subsided.

He licked his lips and grinned, conscious of a tightening across his face.

"How about that, lads," Pete's laugh sounded metallic through the earphones, "He popped his cherry. Guess who'll be buying the drinks tonight?"

The ever-present radio crackled again. Lt. Comdr. Silverman's voice came across wearily. "That was fun, boys, but it cost us. We've got to refuel locally. Pete, where's the nearest detachment?"

"Detachment 4 is aboard the *Springfield County,* on the *Ham Luong.*"

"Good, we'll land there.

The two gunships swung northeast and head for the *USS Springfield County,* a support landing ship, home base to another helicopter detachment on another branch of the river.

In a few minutes they were dropping down and landing. "How about that, Lieutenant" Burman said. "No sand."

"Hell, no. This is Navy country."

The officers headed for the wardroom while the two crewmen remained behind to supervise the refueling and rearming of their craft. After it was done to their satisfaction, they went below to the crew's quarters for some coffee, a ham sandwich and a head call.

In the wardroom the four officers were drinking coffee, finishing up some hot minestrone and looking at some Danish pastries a Filipino steward had brought them. "You guys in the Navy sure know how to live," Howie Martinez was telling Ensign Steve Farkas. I'll bet you don't even have sand in your shaving cream or bugs in your teeth."

Farkas smirked. "No one told you to join the Army. You should have had enough at Benning." The two young officers had trained together and arrived in-country together. The present opportunity to meet and discuss experiences was an unexpected luxury. A short one.

"C'mon, guys," Sam Silverman said, "No time for talk. We've got to get back home. We still have a couple of hours of patrol left." A few minutes later they were preparing to climb into their choppers when Farkas dashed over.

"We've got a scramble. A PBR's been hit on the *Ham Luong*, right opposite *Ben Tre*. An Army L-19 aerial observer reports an estimated 300 VC in the area. There's also a request for a 'medevac' of one of the more seriously wounded PBR crewmen."

As they took off, Fred asked Pete, "*Ben Tra?* We were just there."

"Different spelling, Fred. This is T-R-E. It's further north. Close to *Dong Tam.* Anyhow, the VNs pronounce them different." Fifteen minutes later the *Long Duc* team, joined by a Detachment 4 team from the *Springfield County*, were over the smoking PBR. Fred looked down at the 31-foot fiberglass boat, looking like a toy model of the recreation boat it once was, before being turned into a ship of war, with a pair of M-60 machine guns and a small grenade launcher. Inadequate, he thought, pitifully inadequate for its mission of patrolling the rivers. And yet...

"Heads up, Fred," Pete yelled. "Sam's made a run on the tree line across the river from the town."

Fred saw a thin, spiraling column of purple smoke marking the site Silverman had designated as target zone.

"Got to be careful, here," Pete said. "Sam has to keep his fire light and tight because of the friendlies in the area. Hey, 42's going in. That's Howie's buddy, Farkas. Let's go down and escort. But this time, troops, let's make sure we're wearing our flak vests, hot weather or not."

The gunships hovered over the area, the four men aboard constantly scanning the tree line as the helicopter from the *Springfield County* landed and took the wounded sailor aboard. "They're headed for *Dong Tam*," Pete told Fred. "The Army's got a hospital just up the river. Looks like the cover ship is staying."

"Okay, boys," Sam's voice came in. "Let's hit the area with automatic and rockets. Use "Willy Peter" if you get the chance. We've got to give those PBRs a hand." He turned to Fred. "White Phosphorous works well for spooking the VC."Fred looked down. Two PBRs, now looking more like water beetles in motion, were attempting to approach the burning boat, but were held off by fire from the river bank, the target site Sam had marked.

The three choppers took turns making runs at the enemy site, shooting rockets and M-60 fire into the tree line. Fred experienced the exhilaration again, but was careful to restrict his fire to the area. He was feeling calmer.

"I've got some 'Willy Peter' grenades back here, Mr. Rogers," Burman said.

"Okay, drop a couple, but don't expect too much. The brush is too thick. I'll stall for a second, but make it quick." True to his word he zoomed in low over the area, leaning to the left as the crew chief pulled the pins on two white phosphorous grenades and arched them into the area. A couple of pings on the hull of the craft indicated the return of fire. "Let's get out of here," Pete yelled as they accelerated. From the height of 1,000 feet Fred could see the smoke of one of the "Willy Peter" grenades burning harmlessly on top of a palm tree. There was no indication where the other went.

"Hey, 53! Pete! What the hell are you doing? You drew some fire. I meant rockets. Quit showing off. Fred'll have plenty of chance to get his thrills."

"I read you, Skipper. Sorry."

"No sweat. Good show. The sector advisor has called in some Air Force F-100s for an air strike."

"Great, Skipper! Three thousand feet, huh? The Air Force doesn't understand low-level ground support."

"No matter. It's their show, now. Let's refuel and re-arm *at Ben Tre* while we're here. Just in case. We used up quite a bit."

The three choppers dropped slowly into a clearing on the other side of town. Fred got out, gently touching his feet to the solid ground. A sudden feeling of fatigue came over him; he felt drained. Slowly, he walked around, stretching his cramped leg muscles in long strides.

Pete fell into step beside him. "This is an experience for you, Fred. We don't use this field much. The ARVNs maintain it for us."

"Nice, Pete. I see the ammo hooches and some fuel drums, but where's the fuel tank?"

"You're standing on it, dummy. It's a 10,000 gallon fuel bladder, full of just the stuff we need. Hey, the skipper's waving. You stay here and help with the refueling. Keep an eye on the ARVNs. Make sure they put the rockets in the pods facing in the right direction. Also, make sure they don't walk off with everything inside the craft that isn't tied down. Last time we lost a clipboard and three boxes of C-rats."

Fred walked over and began to load the rockets, assisted and directed by Burman. One of the Vietnamese soldiers was bending down, pulling at something on the ground. Fred walked over and looked at it. It was a thin wire. He followed it over to a group of small fuel drums near the fuel bladder where Sierocki was gassing the ship. He waved at Pete, who was heading toward him. Fred lifted the wire and began following it toward an open field.

Rogers ran after him, breathlessly. "The *Springfield* chopper is coming back from *Dong Tam*. The skipper took two bullets through his main rotor and is returning to *Long Duc*." He looked at Fred. "What've you got there?"

"A wire. Seems to be leading out to the field. Is it some sort of safety evice?"

"Oh, shit," Rogers yelled, pulling out a K-bar from the sheath on his leg. He slashed at the wire, then knocked Fred down, throwing himself down next to him.

The two lay there in the dust for only a minute, though it seemed longer to Fred. Pete raised his hand, then slowly rose, reaching out for the wire and following it, now severed, back to the group of fuel drums. He bent down, kneeling in the sand and brushing it from the wire. His face turned pale as he called back, "Fred! Burman! Sierocki! Over here." The three men rushed to him. He lifted out a small package, about the size and shape of a shoebox, bound with wire. "Sierocki! What is it?"

The airman's eyes narrowed, then widened as he dropped to his knees next to the pilot. "Satchel charge. Command-detonated." He drew in his breath, suddenly. "Is it..?"

"It is. I cut the wire myself. Let's finish up quickly before we find any more gifts. What's that?"

"Looks like a Detachment 6 chopper. Must be from *Dong Tam*," Burman answered.

They returned to the ship and continued loading ammunition. Fred found himself bewildered by the quick turn of events. His chest felt tight and his stomach loose. He was carefully lifting the sixth rocket into the left pod when there was a sharp explosion in the distance and the ground began to shake. He slammed the rocket into place and looked up. Smoke was billowing at the end of the airfield. As he watched, another explosion erupted in front of the first, closer to the still parked choppers.

"Mortar!" someone yelled, as the men ran toward their ships. Two more mortars hit the field, each closer to the helicopters than the previous one. Pete shoved Fred into his seat, then jumped into his own and began spinning the rotor. A mortar exploded to their right.

"Hey!" Burman yelled, "Wait!" A box of ammunition was on the edge of the doorway of the craft, and Burman was still on the ground, pushing it in. Sierocki reached over, grabbing his crew chief by the wrist. Burman, in turn, grabbed Sierocki's wrist and was lifted aboard.

Go!" Sierocki yelled. The craft slowly rose as two more rockets hit the runway. River Ranger 42 suddenly erupted in flames. Fred leaned forward. "We've got to go back. That's Howie's friend."

Pete shook his head. "Forget it. Nothing we can do for them now. The other detachment will return after we've cleared the area. Just concentrate on creaming those bastards."

The radio crackled. "Fifty-three; Sixty-two; this is Forty. I'll take command. The mortars seem to be coming from two kilometers northwest of the field. Let's take it with rocket." More centrifugal force, more cordite, slightly less adrenalin engulfed Fred. Since it was a rocket attack, the rockets being fired by the pilot, he didn't get a chance to fire. He leaned back and observed, feeling somewhat like a moviegoer in the midst of a 3-D happening. He found himself almost detached, watching the entire action from afar. He heard Pete Rogers advise the *Ben Tre* sector advisor of the airfield attack, but it meant nothing. He stared out of the window, observing the ground come up , s u d d e n l y.

"Hey, buddy , wake up." Pete punched him lightly on the arm. Fred turned, staring into Pete's grin. "This *is Dong Tam,* We have five minutes to finish re-arming." In five minutes they had done so. Fred, himself, had loaded five of the seven rockets in the almost empty pod. Pete had fired four during the ambush site attack.

"We're going home solo," Pete said. "The skipper and Howie missed all the excitement. Howie! Someone's got to tell him about Farkas. Though there's a small hope he made it out safely." To Fred, Pete didn't sound very hopeful at all.

Four hours and thirty minutes after taking off on their "routine" mission, they returned to *Long Duc.* Fred looked at his watch, shook it to see if it had stopped, looked at the second hand slowly revolving around the dial, and then shook his head.

"Hey, Fred," Pete yelled after they had landed, "Look here." He pointed to several scratched dents in the shell of the ship, just below the windshield on the co-pilot's side. "You got shot at, Boy." He slapped his leg in an exaggerated gesture, and laughed again. "Yep. Busted your cherry all right. Let's head back to the Admin. hut and see if there's any mail. We've got another mission this afternoon."

The two removed their flak jackets and trudged over to the Administration hut, picked up their mail, then headed for their Quonset hut for some food, some rest, and some talk. As Fred lay in his rack, he looked up into the curved ceiling, seeing palm trees and rocket flashes, smoke columns and whirring blades, seeing River Ranger 42 in flames. He closed his eyes, but the pictures stayed.

In this one day he had seen combat, he had seen camaraderie, he had seen death, and he had seen a disturbing distrust of their Vietnamese allies. He had seen so much and he had seen so little. He was exhausted and he was refreshed. He was sleepy, and he couldn't sleep. He knew so much, yet he still knew so little.

He was on a one-year tour of duty. One year. Fifty-two weeks. And this was the seventh day.

———————————

So, now I come to the most controversial of my stories. It was writ-ten as a class exercise when I was a graduate student at San Diego State University. I was writing about the unrealiable narrator, the person you can't always trust. In this case, he says he remembers very little about the private, but the narration disproves that. However, when writing any story a character goes off on his own, somewhere the author hadn't planned in advance, hence the ending.

ANOTHER HILL TO BE TAKEN

When the kid first joined our unit I knew he was different. I'm not sure how. I don't have his way with words, so this might sound con-fusing; but he was different because he was so much like all these other kids they're drafting out of college. He kept trying to see the world in larger terms, untouched by what he called "nationalistic provincialism."

That's what I mean. I never did understand that. To me, Nationalism is what we fought for in our revolution. To keep us free from foreign domination. And not just us, but the people of South Vietnam. I mean, isn't that what we're here for?

89

The kid, just a private, had been in our outfit for several -weeks. A replacement, you know, and, therefore, an outsider. No, actually, as the sergeant, I was the outsider. That's how it is, now. As we draft more of these college kids, I'm more and more out of it.

I usually ignore them, which is why I didn't get to know this kid very well, until the morning of the battle. I just called him "Private." They promote them so fast these days a guy doesn't get a chance to use the word very often. I like the feel of it on my tongue.

Private. Sarge. The words represent order. I understand that.

As I say, I got to know him a little better before the battle in the *A Shau* Valley, to take some unnamed hill that the enemy took back a week later. Hell! Now I'm talking like he did. I guess he got to me, after all, with all the college crap he spouted.

He said he didn't learn his ideas because of the University but in spite of the University.

"They propagandize us," he told me in that misty dawn, "and they try to socialize us into accepting the establishment; but they don't train us to think.

"This we have to develop on our own. And we do. They're so rigid in their thought processes they haven't had a new thought in years. But for us this is all new. And so we continue to think, even after they expect us to stop,

"But they've discovered a way to insure that, now. A way to keep us from thinking." He sounded bitter.

"How?" I asked. I thought I knew the answer.

"The Army." I did.

"That's always the excuse, isn't it?" I was a bit surprised at the violence of my reaction. I held myself in and went on. "You've had

90

it soft. First you were supported by your folks on the farm you were telling me about. Then you went to school at public expense. Now you're asked for something in return. Just to defend your country."

As I spoke, the tropic chill began to dissipate. I wiped a bead of sweat from my upper lip and took off my camouflage jacket. It gave me some time to put some words together. I wasn't going to admit I'm not too happy about being here, myself. But for different reasons.

I looked around. At the kid, at the jungle surrounding us, at the distant hills—ours? theirs? Who the hell knows? Or cares? Certainly not the politicians who run this war—and then at my hands. I took a couple of deep breaths and looked at the kid again—young, innocent, sloppily dressed in the olive-green common to armies around the world. It's supposed to resemble the bush, but it never does. Nature can't copy the unimaginativeness of men.

I shook my head, hoping I could shake the thoughts. I looked at him, again. He had an eager vulnerable look. Why do they keep sending me kids like this? They don't last. The survival instinct isn't there. I knew he wouldn't last. I also knew I had to say something. Pretend to myself? *No!* I shook my head, again.

I looked at the kid. "Do you understand what I'm saying?"

"I don't know, Sarge. Do you? You say something, then there's a long pause while you look all around. What are you looking at, Sarge."

Your death, Boy! Or someone like you. Before and again. I shook my head. "I'm talking about patriotism. About freedom. Do you want them on your folk's farm? Do you want those foreigners raping your sister?" Just for a moment I had a twinge of regret at using that tired argument.

"No, and I don't want to rape anyone's sister, either. But am I protecting my country, here? This far from home? We're here to save the people from foreign ideologies. To promote something called national self-determination. The right to make their own decisions without pressure. Then why do they hate us? Why do they accuse us of committing atrocities? Of massacring their villagers? Why do we commit atrocities? Massacre their villagers? Why do I feel such contempt for their weakness? Why don't I hate the enemy, as I should? With his funny-looking eyes and strange smell?"

"You ask too many questions, Private. They'll get you in trouble. In fact, if we weren't getting ready for the big push, that kind of talk could get you time in the stockade."

The big push. The monsoons had turned the mountain lowlands into a swamp more usually associated with the Delta. As the sun came up, we began to move out.

To say it was hot is to understate the situation in the cruelest way. But after my little conversation with the Private, I almost welcomed it. Kids who doubt their country's honor are difficult to understand. Jungle heat is much easier to put into words.

Calling it miserable describes a surface condition hinting at nothing of the depth of feeling. There's a sticky, drippy, breezeless mélange of rotting leaves, stale water vapor and sandy flying insects you're forced to breathe.

You're not even allowed the dubious luxury of a short cough. Your only relief, such as it is, is in unvoiced curses. Fortunately, I'm very good at that.

Crawling down my back was something I devoutly hoped was sweat.

There wasn't much time for thinking about it, because suddenly a shot was fired by one of our advance scouts and we were in the midst of a battle. I was in my element.

In a combat situation, everyone is expected to remain calm. This is more important in the event of a surprise attack such as this one. But there are many ways of staying calm. I have no trouble because the situation holds no mystery, only familiar problems for which I have the answers. I remained calm from knowledge and experience.

Surprisingly enough, the kids who are completely green can remain calm, too. But their calm is based on lack of experience. They don't realize the extent of the attack, the imminent danger they face, the possibility of their position being overrun.

Lack of experience carries its own tranquilizing aura. If a kid is in his first firefight, he hasn't seen anyone killed or even wounded and still has a feeling of permanence.

As the battle diminished to its usual cautious first-lull stalemate while both sides regrouped, I found myself–I don't know why–thinking of the Private. This was his second action, when he knows enough to be scared, but not enough to conquer this fear. It's a time when panic always brushes the edge of consciousness, and the calmness, when it comes, if it comes, is forced, rigid and tightly gripped.

I went looking for him. I'd never done that before. I had always looked out for *all* my troops, but never looked for just *one*. It's bad business. These replacements just aren't around long enough to make any difference.

But I went looking for him. I found him, alone, manning a machine gun between the bodies of a couple of his friends. One was dead, the other soon would be.

"How are you, Private?" I yelled.

"Alive," he laughed. "Alive and fighting for Freedom." His voice was hard and a bit brittle. I listened to the distant artillery fire. Theirs? Ours? I waited.

"Sarge." The shift in tone was abrupt, but not unexpected.

"Sarge?" The plea was stronger. I knew what was coming.

"Sarge!"

He was beginning to panic. I figured I'd better say something. "Yeah?"

"I'm scared."

"Sure."

"More scared than I was before." He was getting a tone of annoyance -in his voice, but the whine was fading away.

It was time for words of wisdom from the Sarge. I chose them carefully. "Private, that's normal. I know you've heard that everyone is scared the first time he goes into battle. You've been through that. But now you're disappointed in still being scared.

"I'll tell you about fear. And it won't be like your college professors tell you. It's not intellectual. It's gut and mind mixed up. At first you're afraid of being afraid; and then you taste the real fear, itself, as you're looking for an enemy who's looking for you, and you both secretly hope you'll never meet. And then, one day, you're not afraid, and that scares you even more, because then you're afraid of yourself."

"Sergeant, you're eloquent."

94

I uttered my favorite syllable. The kid was mocking me, so his crisis was over. For a while. "Private, you bug me."

"Just so I have some effect on someone. Maybe that's my goal in life." The kid was okay.

I walked away. I had to take charge of the troops. Some fool second lieutenant, my fourth company commander in as many months, had gotten his head blown off trying to *see* what was going on instead of just feeling and listening. Another kid. Like the Private.

When I next saw the Private, he was still at the machine gun between his two buddies. But now, he was no longer alone.

For a moment I tried remembering what his last words to me were, but couldn't. I decided they weren't important. Words never are. They start you thinking about things, but it never lasts.

We had to abandon our position and leave the bodies behind. So he didn't even get his wish–to be buried on his folk's farm. But what's the difference? The question remains: what good will all those grand ideas do him now, buried–if he is buried–wherever he is?

What good will those grand ideas do his parents on their farm in that little village just north of Hanoi? What good will they do any of us?

I don't know.

What I do know is that there's another hill to be taken.

—

1974

PHOTOGRAPHS

- Dick relaxing after a June PBR trip along the Cambodian Border

- Navy Correspondence ID

- The roof of Naval Headquarters during the TET Offensive

- Dick with members of Marine Advisory Team 43

- Riding in a P-3 Orion over the coast of South Vietnam

- A rare smile

U.S. NAVY CORRESPONDENT

PUBLIC AFFAIRS OFFICE, COMMANDER U.S. NAVAL FORCES, VIETNAM

Richard S. ROSE
TYPED NAME

384 10 79
SERVICE NUMBER

JOCS (E-8)
GRADE

SIGNATURE OF CORRESPONDENT

45
CARD NUMBER

OCT 1 1968
EXPIRATION DATE

LCDR C.M. GAMMELL, USN

Rooftop of Naval Forces Vietnam, Headquarters, Saigon
JOCS Rose, Phjotographers, and Journalists at GQ
2/2/67, VietCong Tet Offensive

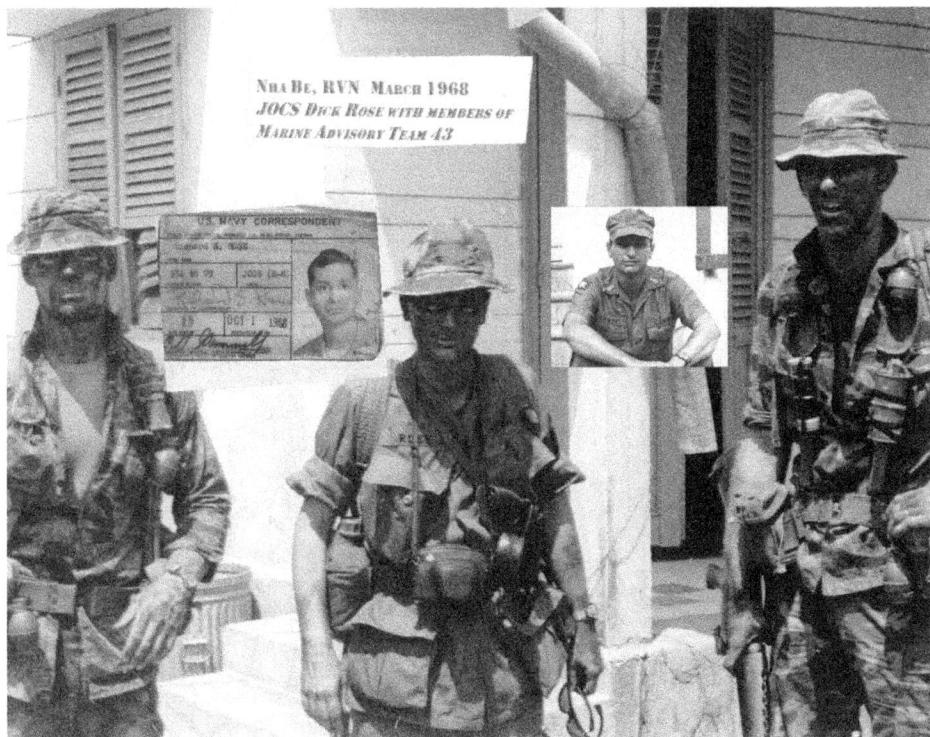

NHA BE, RVN MARCH 1968
JOCS DICK ROSE WITH MEMBERS OF
MARINE ADVISORY TEAM 43

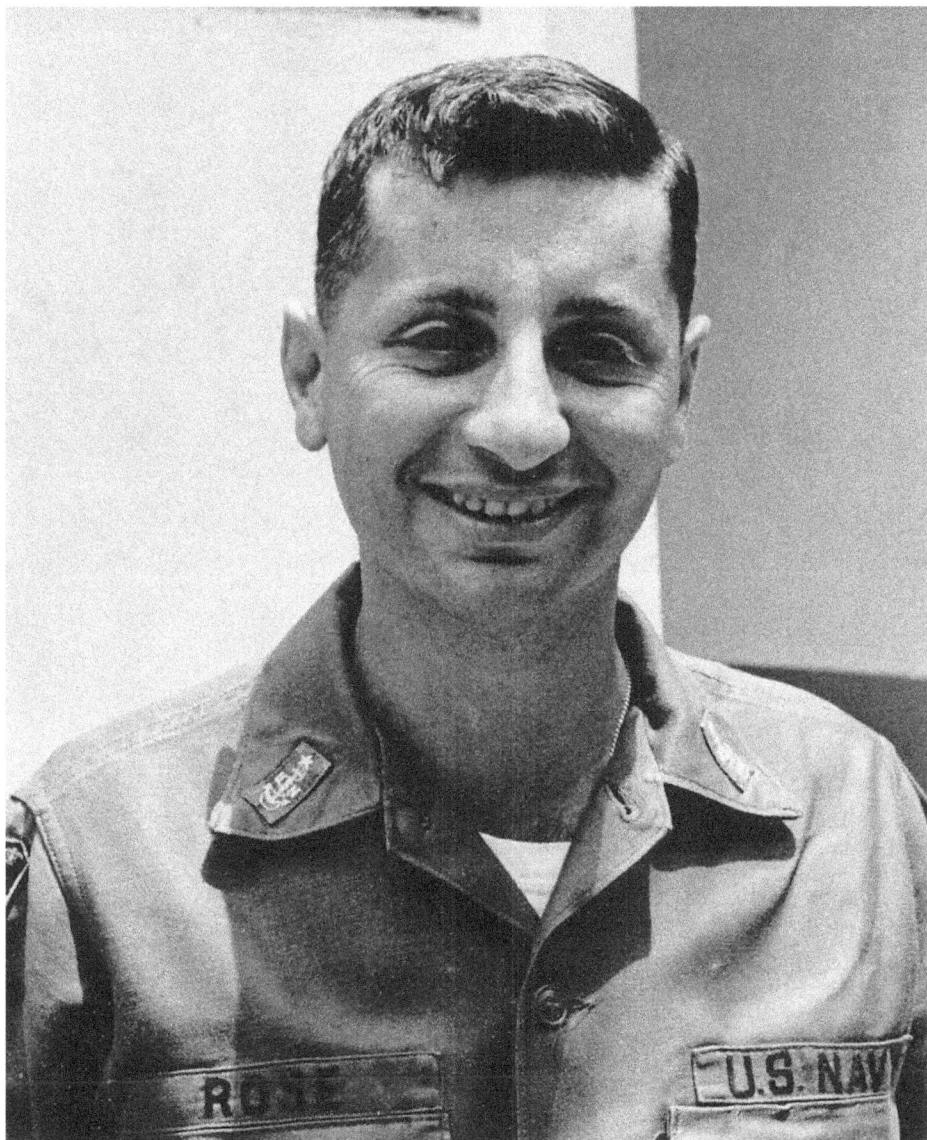

www.ingramcontent.com/pod-product-compliance
Lightning Source LLC
Chambersburg PA
CBHW070521030426
42337CB00016B/2056